AN ODYSSEY ROUND ODYSSEUS

Beaty Rubens is the producer of the BBC Radio 4 series
An Odyssey Round Odysseus. She studied Classics at Emmanuel
College, Cambridge. She has worked as a researcher and producer
for many Radio 4 programmes including *The Memory of Troy*.

Oliver Taplin is the presenter of the BBC Radio 4 series
An Odyssey Round Odysseus. He is the author of *The Stagecraft
of Aeschylus* and *Greek Tragedy in Action*, and has published
numerous articles on Greek tragedy, comedy and epic. He was
the academic consultant on the television series *Greek Fire*
and wrote the accompanying book.

AN ODYSSEY ROUND
ODYSSEUS

The man and his story traced through time and place

Beaty Rubens and Oliver Taplin

BBC BOOKS

FRONTISPIECE] *Detail of
Jan Brueghel the Elder and
Hendrick de Clerck's painting
of Odysseus and Calypso
(reproduced in full on
pages 74–5).*

*Published by BBC Books
a division of BBC Enterprises Limited
Woodlands, 80 Wood Lane, London W12 0TT*

First published 1989
© *Beaty Rubens and Oliver Taplin 1989*

ISBN 0 563 20783 3

*Printed and bound in Great Britain by
Richard Clay Ltd, Bungay, Suffolk*

100624.3907

Contents

Introduction

To make a series of radio programmes and a book about Odysseus –
it was an irresistible challenge. What was more, travel was written
into the budget, travel for work, but work not inconsistent with
swimming in the Aegean, eating grilled fish and drinking retsina.

Our aim from the start was to explore the manifold character of
Odysseus and try to explain his enduring popularity. Homer's
Odysseus is the archetype, but not the only one: it is, we believe, of
the essence of our man that he has kept on recurring in various
guises across the centuries of art and literature since Homer. The
goal of Homer's Odysseus was Ithaca: the goal of ours was to be
Odysseus himself.

So our interest does not lie in trying to follow in the wake of
Odysseus, as though we were trying to retrace a real journey. In any
case Calypso's island and the cave of the Cyclops are not real locations to be found on any map: what intrigues us, rather, is the
relationship between reality, poetry and imagination. Even Homer's
Troy and Ithaca, let alone the places of Odysseus' wanderings, do
not exactly fit all the facts of reality. What we suspected, however,
was that elements of the real world had been combined and transformed by the creative mind. In a similar way we came to feel more
and more that Homer transformed the historical realities of his own
day into a poetry which could far outlast them.

What, then, was the point of going abroad at all? This wasn't
television, so what were we going to find – what, indeed were we
going to look for – that a good library in Oxford and the BBC Sound
Archives couldn't supply? Our itinerary was more than mere self-
justification: it encapsulated our ideas about how we might succeed
in the project. We were going in search of Homer's world, of the
world around him while he was creating his perennial figure. Our
feeling – and this intuition was excitingly confirmed on location –
was that this archetype was somehow a product of the poet's time
and of the places he knew. And we hoped that the discoveries we
made would be transferable to the Odysseuses of other places and
times.

Our three key locations were Ithaca, Odysseus' home; Troy, the
scene of his heroic triumphs; and Cape Maleia where he was blown
off course on his return journey. Our search for the realities of
Homer's times took us, accompanied by the historian Oswyn
Murray, to Chios and Smyrna, both traditionally associated with
Homer, and to Mycene, Lefkandí, Eretria, Corinth and Corfu, places
which illuminate aspects of his present and of his past and future.

Wherever we went we found traces of Odysseus – not footprints, but fragments or touches which in different ways stirred the imagination and took us a little further in our circumnavigation.

While travelling round Odysseus, the producer (Beaty Rubens) worked on the tapes and on shaping the programmes, while the presenter (Oliver Taplin) worked on the translations that appear in this book, and which Brian Glover was to perform on radio. It has been a fascinating challenge to create translations which are primarily to be *heard*. Anyone who reads them out loud will soon see the principles by which each line is divided into two groups of sound patterns. A list of all passages translated in this book is given on page 168. On pages 170–1 there is a 'cast list' of all the important names in Homer, with a brief reminder of their place in the story of the *Iliad* and the events at Troy, or of the *Odyssey* and Odysseus' return home.

We set off in the spirit of Tennyson's eternal voyager:

The long day wanes: the slow moon climbs: the deep
Moans round with many voices. Come, my friends,
'Tis not too late to seek a newer world.
Push off, and sitting well in order smite
The sounding furrows. . .

BR, OT
February–June 1989

Acknowledgements

Many have helped in various ways in the course of this voyage of tape-recorder, pen and word-processor. Oswyn Murray has made an especially important contribution both to the programmes and the book. We should like to thank Frances Abraham, John Cook, Anthea Dobry, Shane Fletcher, Merilyn Harris, Tony Harrison, George Huxley, Clive Griffin, John Kelly, Susan Kennedy, Manfred Korfmann, Robin Osborne, Enid Rubens, Richard Rutherford, Anthony Snodgrass, Tim Suter, Sarantis Symeonoglou and Suzanne Webber. Tony Harrison has kindly allowed us to quote on page 101 from his unpublished *Trojan Women* and Angela Scholar has translated the du Bellay for us on pages 152 and 153.

Acknowledgement is also due to the following:

Anvil Press Poetry for permission to quote from 'Reflections on a foreign line of verse' in the *Collected Poems of George Seferis*, translated by Edmund Keeley and Philip Sherrard.
The Bodley Head for permission to quote from James Joyce, *Ulysses*.
The Estate of Jorge Luis Borges for permission to quote from 'The Maker' and 'Ars Poetica' in *Selected Poems 1923–1967*, copyright © Jorge Luis Borges.
Cambridge University Press for permission to quote from David Constantine, *Early Greek Travellers and the Hellenic Ideal*.
The Estate of C. V. Cavafy for permission to quote from 'Ithaca' in the *Collected Poems of C. P. Cavafy*, translated by John Mavrogordato.
Faber and Faber for permission to quote from 'Day of Returning' in *Louis MacNeice Collected Poems*, edited by E. R. Dodds.
David Higham Associates Ltd for permission to quote from Dante, *The Divine Comedy*, translated by Dorothy L. Sayers.
Tony Robinson and Richard Curtis for permission to quote from *Odysseus – The Greatest Hero Of Them All*.
Suzanne Vega and Rondor Music (London) Ltd for permission to quote from the song 'Calypso' from her album *Solitude Standing*.

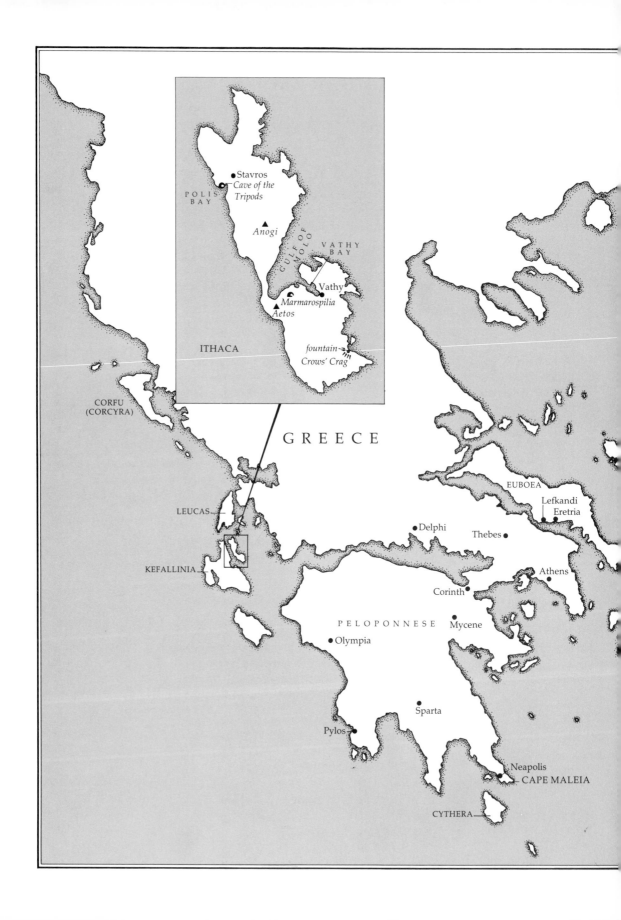

POLIS BAY

● Stavros
○ *Cave of the Tripods*

▲ *Anogi*

G U L F   O F   M O L O

V A T H Y   B A Y

● Vathy

▲ *Marmarospilia*
Aetos

ITHACA

fountain
Crows' Crag

CORFU
(CORCYRA)

G R E E C E

EUBOEA

● Lefkandi
● Eretria

LEUCAS

● Delphi

Thebes ●

KEFALLINIA

● Athens

Corinth ●

P E L O P O N N E S E

● Mycene

● Olympia

● Sparta

Pylos ●

● Neapolis
CAPE MALEIA

CYTHERA

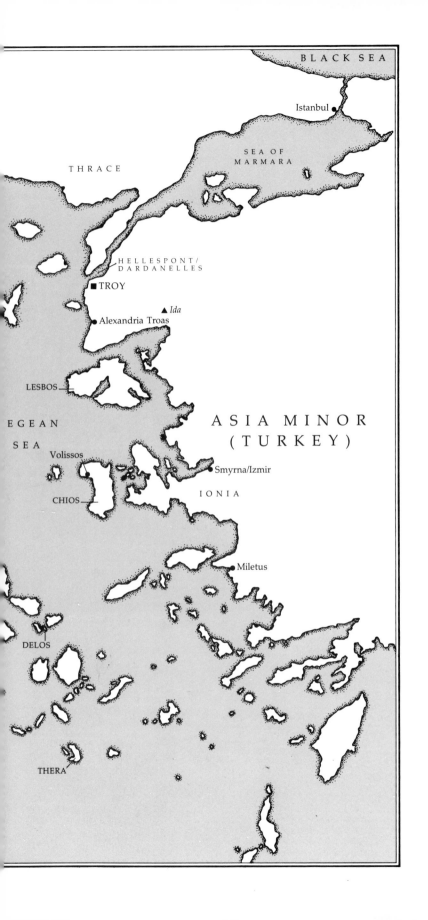

BLACK SEA

Istanbul

THRACE

SEA OF
MARMARA

HELLESPONT/
DARDANELLES

■ TROY

▲ *Ida*

● Alexandria Troas

LESBOS

ASIA MINOR
(TURKEY)

E G E A N

S E A

Volissos

● Smyrna/Izmir

CHIOS

I O N I A

● Miletus

DELOS

THERA

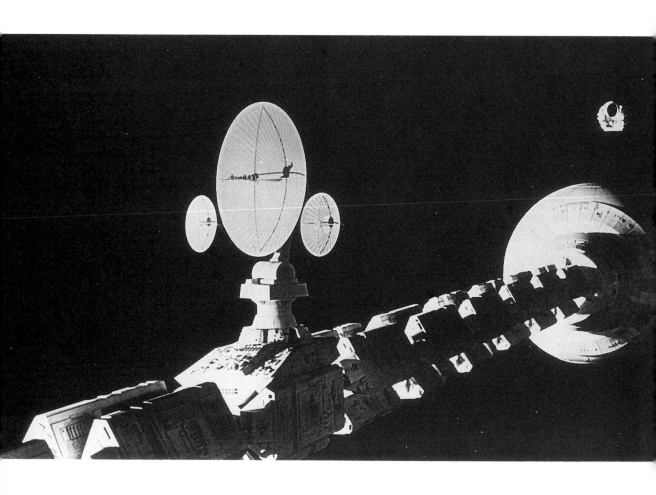

1 ON THE TRACK OF ODYSSEUS

And he began to read the Odyssey, which of all books
spoke to him most vividly across the gulfs of time.

    Arthur C. Clarke, 2001 A Space Odyssey

The spaceship Discovery *from Stanley Kubrick's film* 2001 A Space Odyssey.

'Dogs, you were so damned sure   I'd never come home from Troy'.

A single line sums up Homer's *Odyssey*. When the moment comes, Odysseus does not need to trumpet his name: these words are enough to identify the vagrant on the threshold, and to transform him into the great avenger.

Odysseus has returned to the island of Ithaca after twenty years away, to find his house full of young men carousing at his expense and hoping to marry his wife Penelope. Disguised as an old beggar, he has seen for himself that they are behaving so outrageously that they – and above all their ringleader Antinous – deserve death.

Odysseus does not reveal himself, even to his wife. On the very day of his return she decides to hold a contest to find a new husband. The man who will win her must string the great bow that Odysseus left at home when he went to Troy, and fire it, as he used to, through a row of axes. One by one the suitors fail, and in the end the old beggar is allowed to try his hand:

>   Once subtle Odysseus
> had handled the whole bow   and looked it all over,
> then with the same ease   as an expert at poetry
> and lyre-playing   stretches a new string,
> and fixes the flexible   sheep-gut round both pegs,
> so without any strain   he strung the great bow.
> Next he plucked it with his   fingers, testing the string,
> and it sang out sweetly,   like the call of the swallow.
> Then he picked up an arrow   lying loose on the table –
> the rest remained   inside the quiver,
> though the suitors were   soon to taste them.
> Stretching flights and string   back to the bridge of the bow,
> he didn't even stand,   but taking his aim,
> shot the arrow straight   winging through all the axes.

One moment a beggar, the next a poet, and then a great man of action: Homer here conjures up the archetype of the subtle, adaptable man that makers have recreated across the centuries.

Subtle Odysseus   stripped the rags from his legs
and leaped up onto the threshold,   brandishing bow and quiver
packed with its arrows;   then poured all of them out
in front of his feet,   and said to the suitors:
'So this first test   has been properly passed.
Now I shall shoot   at an untouched target,
to see if I can score first hit,   with Apollo's help.'
He aimed his arrow-head   straight at Antinous,
who was half-lifting   a golden goblet
with double handles,   and had it in his hands,
to taste the vintage,   with no thought of slaughter.
Who would think that one man   among many men at their feasting,
however brave, could ever   strike him down in dark death?
Taking careful aim   Odysseus shot through the throat;
the arrow-point pierced   the tender part of his neck.
He slumped to one side,   the cup dropped from his grip,
and a spurting jet   of mortal blood gushed out
through his nostrils.   With a convulsive jerk of his foot
he overturned his table,   and the food poured onto the floor –
the bread and roasted meat   were blood-stained and spoiled.
The suitors shouted out   when they saw Antinous down;
they started from their seats   and stood throughout the hall,
and scolded Odysseus   with words full of fury:
'Men are the wrong mark   for your arrows, stranger,
you've won your last contest,   and your sheer death is sure.
The man you've just struck   was the pick of Ithaca;
so your corpse will be carrion   for the vultures of this island.'
That's what each supposed,   since they assumed he had hit
the man by mistake –   the fools didn't realise the truth
that the rope-ends of death   were fastened over every one.
Subtle Odysseus   said with an angry frown:
'Dogs, you were so damned sure   I'd never come home from Troy . . .'

THE MAN OF TWISTS AND TURNS

Without its wonderful storytelling, the *Odyssey*, and Odysseus with it, would never have survived. The story can still enthrall huge audiences. In 1986 *Odysseus – The Greatest Hero Of Them All* won the Royal Television Society's award for Best Children's Programme. This rollicking, masculine retelling by Tony Robinson has captured the imagination of millions of children – and adults:

Odysseus scattered the arrows on the floor in front of him.

'We underestimated you,' said the pimply suitor, his voice edged with fear. 'I drink your health.' He lifted his goblet, but he never drank. Odysseus' arrow went through his throat like a hot knife through butter. He slumped on to the table, his dead head resting on a pig with an orange in its mouth.

'Kill him!' yelled the suitors, and rushed to the wall for the weapons.

Henry Fuseli's dramatic sketch of Odysseus' Revenge on the Suitors *(1802), captioned with the Greek for 'he stripped the rags from his legs, and leaped up onto the threshold'. This scene is discussed on page 149.*

Then a voice behind them froze them where they stood. 'You terrorised my wife. You ruined my country. You plundered my house. You abused my servants. Now prepare to die.'

Slowly, slowly, they turned to see who it was who had so confidently condemned them to death. At first they thought it was just the tramp, and their spirits rose an inch or two. But then the tramp tore off his hood, and their spirits sank a mile. Because in front of them stood Odysseus, King of Ithaca. He was home at last, after twenty years. And he was very angry.

The colour drained from the suitors' faces and the weasely suitor dropped to his knees. 'Odysseus,' he squealed, 'We've behaved abominably. I'm truly, truly sorry. Gosh, I'm sorry. I mean, so incredibly sorry . . . really, really sorry. But, hey, welcome home.'

On our Odyssey we found we could never pin Odysseus down: we were forever tracking him through time and place, always changing and elusive, yet always unmistakably Odysseus. His changeability is there in the first verse of the poem:

ἄνδρα μοι ἔννεπε, Μοῦσα, πολύτροπον . . .

The man, my Muse,   tell of that man of twists and turns,
who wandered the wide world   after he'd sacked Troy's citadel.
He saw all kinds of country   and fathomed deep men's minds,
he bore all sorts of troubles   upon the deep ocean,
struggling for survival   and to bring his comrades home.

Odysseus, that man of twists and turns, weaves his way subtly through the human imagination – across 'the roads of the ocean' and along 'the pathways of poetry', in Homer's phrases. He is an insinuator, a spellbinder, endlessly transformed in art and literature.

It is part of Homer's poetic technique that his main characters have their own recurrent epithets, or labels – 'fast-footed Achilles', 'Hector of the glinting crest', and so forth. Those most commonly applied to Odysseus are 'the man of much subtlety and stealth', *polumechanos* (twenty-two times), 'of much grit and control', *polutlas* (thirty-eight times), and 'of much craft and cunning', *polumetis* (no fewer than eighty-one times). These three phrases describe Odysseus in a nutshell, while leaving his character variable.

Even his name is shifting. In the texts of Homer he is Odysseus or Odyseus. In many early records he is Olysseus, and yet other versions have been found: Olytteus, Olyxeus, Oulixes, Olyxes. In Italy his name took the form Ulyxes or Ulysses, which is what it became in Latin, and hence in the classical Western tradition. So for Shakespeare or Tennyson, or even for James Joyce, educated a hundred years ago, he remained Ulysses. Twentieth-century taste has returned to ancient Greece and restored to him his name of Odysseus.

Homer's versatile figure is on the whole an amiable and admirable man. He is often recalled as he was in the days before his departure to Troy, the Good King 'fair as a father' in a well-ordered society. As James Joyce remarked to his friend Frank Budgen:

> He is son to Laertes, father to Telemachus, husband to Penelope, lover of Calypso, companion in arms of the Greek warriors around Troy, and king of Ithaca. He was subjected to many trials, but with wisdom and courage came through them all.

THE ULYSSES THEME

In this book we set out to explore not only the original *Odyssey*, its poet, his time and place, but also all the transformations of the poem and of Odysseus/Ulysses that appear in other places and in later times. In almost every century of the twenty-five and more that have passed since Homer first told the story, Odysseus and Troy and Ithaca have been recreated in one shape or another. These range from a simple retelling to a refashioning, through the artist's personal response, which speaks afresh to a particular contemporary audience.

This perpetual recurrence provoked a question from the Italian novelist Italo Calvino, which he posed in a newspaper article in 1981 (translated into English in *The Literature Machine* in 1988):

> If I read the *Odyssey* I read Homer's text, but I cannot forget all that the adventures of Ulysses have come to mean in the course of the centuries, and I cannot help wondering if those meanings were implicit in the text, or whether they are encrustations or distortions or expansions.

We certainly do not see all the many Odysseuses as encrustations or distortions, but rather as new growth. They are like the fruiting of a very ancient tree: the trunk remains, the olives are new every year.

Of the harvests through the years – by Sophocles, Dante, Monteverdi, Tennyson and many others – one from the present century beyond all doubt takes its place with the greatest of them: James Joyce's novel *Ulysses*, published in 1922. 'Novel', however, seems hardly the right word – 'pantechnicon' might be more appropriate. It is a book that sometimes seems more joked about than read. In 1968 Cilla Black said of it: 'It cost me thirty-five shillings, and I got stuck on the first page. I think that's disgusting, don't you? No, not the contents, I mean writing a book so that people can't understand it.' It has, on the other hand, been seen as the founding work of modern literature. In his review in *The Dial* in 1923 T. S. Eliot wrote:

> Mr Joyce's parallel use of the *Odyssey* . . . has the importance of a scientific discovery. No one else has built a novel upon such a foundation before: it has never been necessary. . . . Instead of the narrative method, we may use the mythical method. It is, I seriously believe, a step toward making the modern world possible for art.

Joyce was himself aware of the awesomeness of his undertaking: 'The most beautiful, all-embracing theme is that of the *Odyssey*,' he once said to a pupil in Zurich. 'It is greater, more human, than that of Hamlet, Don Quixote, Dante, Faust . . .' He went on 'I am almost afraid to treat such a theme; it's overwhelming.'

Ulysses is a big book, but its 'hero' – again hardly the right word – is a little man, Leopold Bloom, a Jewish advertising agent who lives in Dublin with a wife of doubtful virtue. Yet seasoned travellers will still recognise Odysseus, even though he is in heavy disguise. One of Bloom's acquaintances says of him:

> He's a cultured allroundman, Bloom is . . . He's not one of your common or garden . . . you know . . . There's a touch of the artist about old Bloom.

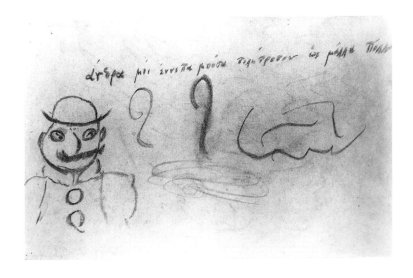

James Joyce himself sketched his 'hero' Leopold Bloom in 1920, while he was writing Ulysses. *He has also written out the first line of the* Odyssey *in Greek.*

There's a touch of the artist about Odysseus when he strings his bow.

Another Dubliner, W. B. Stanford, wrote the great book about the adaptations of Odysseus in later literature. *The Ulysses Theme* combines sympathetic criticism with extraordinarily wide reading (though some Odysseuses have escaped even his capacious trawl: Ezra Pound's 'epic' poem *Cantos*, for example, is a kind of journey to the Underworld starting from a direct citation of the *Odyssey*).

In modern times Odysseus has not been restricted to print. As early as 1905 the French pioneer Georges Méliès made a film, *L'Ile de Calypso*. Mario Camerini's *Ulisse* (1954) is agreed to be one of the better epic films. ('There's a simple definition of the epic film,' said Charlton Heston. 'It's the easiest kind of picture to make badly.') It stars Kirk Douglas and Sylvana Mangano, who plays both Penelope and the temptress Calypso.

And the literary transformations have gone on since Stanford hauled in his net. These range from Nobel Prize-winning authors

Kirk Douglas as Odysseus, with his crew turned into pigs by Circe, in Mario Camerini's epic film Ulisse *(1954).*

such as Thomas Mann and George Seferis to the writers of children's books. In Richard Adams' *Watership Down* the wanderings of the rabbit-hero Hazel and his companions bring them first to a warren of lotus-eaters; later Hazel is transported in a car (a 'hrududu') like Odysseus on the magic ship of the Phaeacians.

At a more serious level, take Jorge Luis Borges, the great Argentinian writer who died in 1986. Homer was always important for him; and when his eyes began to fail during the 1950s, he turned his thoughts to the blind bard Phemius in the *Odyssey*, and to the legend that Homer himself was blind. This inspired the short story, a kind of prose-poem, *The Maker*. The Maker comes to understand why, as he goes blind, the memories of his past become so vivid:

> In this nighttime of his mortal eyes into which he was now descending . . . he already divined (because he was already ringed in by) a rumour of hexameters and glory, a rumour of men defending a shrine which the gods would not save, and of black ships roaming the seas in search of a loved island, the rumour of the Odysseys and the Iliads it was his destiny to sing, and to leave resounding forever in mankind's hollow memory.

Borges also responded to the *Odyssey*'s concern with poetry. He turned Ithaca into a symbol of artistry in his poem *Ars Poetica*:

> To see in death sleep, and in the sunset
> A sad gold – such is poetry –
> Which is immortal and poor. Poetry
> Returns like the dawn and the sunset. . . .
>
> They say that Ulysses, sated with marvels,
> Wept tears of love at the sight of his Ithaca,
> Green and humble. Art is that Ithaca
> Of green eternity, not of marvels.

KING OF CROOKS

Although Homer's Odysseus is on the whole an amiable and admirable man, other ancient Greek versions tell some not so nice stories about him; and these have contributed to his reappearances over the centuries. The Greek tragedians, especially in the fifth century BC, often put Odysseus in an unfavourable light.

One such story tells of his cunning before he even went to Troy. When Menelaus, Helen's deserted husband, came to Ithaca with his clever assistant Palamedes to recruit Odysseus for the expedition against Troy, they found him apparently mad, in rags, ploughing with an ox and an ass under the same yoke, and throwing salt over his shoulder. Palamedes took the baby Telemachus and put him in the furrow ahead: Odysseus stopped, and was thus exposed as sane. James Joyce, who in 1914 was avoiding conscription by remaining in Switzerland, observed to Frank Budgen, 'Don't forget he was a war-dodger. He might never have taken arms and gone to Troy, but the Greek recruiting sergeant was too clever for him.'

The story of how Palamedes unmasked Odysseus' feigned madness, painted by Heywood Hardy in 1874.

Odysseus got his revenge: at Troy he forged a letter from King Priam offering a bribe to betray the Greeks, and planted gold in Palamedes' tent. So his rival was stoned to death. The versions of this unsavoury story by the Athenian dramatists are lost; but Plato alludes to it in the *Apology*, his dramatisation of the real-life tragedy of Socrates' trial and condemnation to death. Socrates says that, if there is an after-life, he will be able to meet all sorts of people:

> It would be an especially interesting experience for me to meet Palamedes and Ajax and any other heroes of the old days who met their death through an unfair judgement.

Odysseus was discreditably involved in the death of Ajax as well. When Achilles, the greatest fighter among the Greeks, was killed by Paris, his armour, made by the god Hephaestus, was to go to the most deserving of the Greeks. Only two considered themselves worthy: Odysseus, by one means or another, defeated Ajax who, in bitter disappointment, killed himself. The Roman poet Ovid in his *Metamorphoses* (written at the beginning of the first century AD) turned this contest into a great debate, which became so well known in the Renaissance that it was a standard exercise in grammar schools for boys to compose their own case for each side. Ajax's speech is blunt and brief: he is a man of action – he fought Hector single-handed, for example. Odysseus works by stealth, Ajax says; and he was responsible for the death of Palamedes and the abandonment of Philoctetes on the way to the war. Odysseus' reply is tinged with hypocrisy: 'he pretended to brush the tears from his eyes,' says

Ovid. Ajax only fought Hector, Odysseus then claims, because his name was drawn by lot after he was the ninth to volunteer: whereas in Homer, Ajax was, in fact, the fourth. It was Odysseus who was the ninth and last. Brains, he insists, are far superior to brawn.

It is the heritage of this Odysseus which is proudly claimed by Richard of Gloucester in Shakespeare's *Henry VI* Part 3:

> I'll play the orator as well as Nestor,
> Deceive more slily than Ulysses could,
> And, like a Sinon, take another Troy.
> I can add colours to the chameleon,
> Change shapes with Proteus for advantages,
> And set the murderous Machiavel to school.

This cup, decorated by the artist Douris in Athens in the early fifth century BC, shows the voting in the contest between Odysseus and Ajax for the armour of the dead Achilles. The goddess Athena indicates that Odysseus is the winner.

The contest between Odysseus and Ajax, which Ovid treats with witty sophistication, becomes high tragedy in Sophocles' *Ajax*. The noble hero actually throws himself onto his sword on stage. Ajax sees Odysseus as his arch enemy and as an utterly unscrupulous double crosser; but in fact Odysseus feels pity for his fate and stands up for Ajax against the petty vindictiveness of the other Greek leaders.

Near the end of his long life Sophocles created another Odysseus in his *Philoctetes*. This is perhaps the most villainous portrayal in the

ABOVE] *This evocation of the agony of Philoctetes, cast away with his festering foot by the other Greeks on the way to Troy, is the work of David Scott (1840).*

RIGHT] *Declan Donnellan's Cheek By Jowl production of Sophocles' Philoctetes in 1989. Charlie Roe plays a ruthless Odysseus in impeccable naval uniform.*

whole tradition. Philoctetes, who owns the magic bow of Heracles, has been marooned by Odysseus and the others on a desert island; now he is needed if Troy is ever to fall, and Odysseus is sent to fetch him. Philoctetes would shoot him on sight if he could, so Odysseus uses Neoptolemus, the young and still innocent son of Achilles, as his bait. He has to persuade him that ends justify means:

> I know, my boy, it's not inborn in you
> to talk crooked and work with treachery;
> yet all the same success feels sweet to grasp,
> so see it through. We can shine with virtue
> some other time; for now give me yourself
> for one brief day's worth of disgrace – and then
> for all the rest of time your reputation
> can be the last word in integrity.

In the end, despite the success of the Odyssean method, Neoptolemus' better nature wins through; he chooses integrity rather than success, and comes clean with Philoctetes, thus nearly exposing Odysseus to one of the deadly arrows. Odysseus runs for safety, utterly humiliated, after the briefest appearance in the whole of Greek tragedy.

Philoctetes seems a very modern play. The Odysseus who plausibly justifies double-dealing is a familiar figure in the world of the free-market economy; and the dilemma of Neoptolemus still faces many young people. But this Odysseus is not to be found only in the capitalist world. One of the most successful of all modern German plays since Bertholt Brecht is the *Philoktetes* of the East German playwright, Heiner Müller, first performed in 1968. In his version, which has a sophisticated relationship with Sophocles' tragedy, Odysseus is the utterly cynical operator, manipulating votes and work forces, and prepared to tell any lie whatsoever, provided it advances the interest of the Party.

Talking of parties, we have enjoyed the thought of inviting all the many Odysseuses and Ulysseses to a huge reunion. They would not recognise each other, they are so different; and they would all be in various disguises, fully occupied with telling each other lies about themselves.

Yet, for all their variety, there is a peculiar coherence about them. Behind each of his many guises lurks the figure round whom we trace our Odyssey. The key to this unity in multiplicity lies in Homer's original. Homer's Odysseus turns up in so many shapes and puts on so many acts; he can turn his hand to almost any skill. He is good at being a carpenter, a sailor, a beggar, a ruler, a bowman. And Homer pays him the greatest compliment by having him compared to a poet.

> There is such charm   in your words and such wisdom:
> you have told your tale   as enchantingly as a poet.

A watercolour by Edward Lear (famous for his nonsense rhymes) of the harbour and town of Vathý in Ithaca, painted in 1863.

ITHACA, GREEN AND HUMBLE

Odysseus returns home to Ithaca. The island of Itháki, as it is called in modern Greek, is not remarkable today. It has only five villages and fewer than 4000 inhabitants. There are some pretty patches of greenery, and in spring the wild flowers scatter colour on even the most mountainous and barren slopes. And most of Ithaca is mountainous and barren. The only way of getting there is by ferry, and the island's most striking physical feature is the one that impresses visitors on arrival: the long gulf which reaches like a finger into the core of the island. At the end of this is the main modern town, Vathý, which means 'deep', because the gulf comes so far into the land. The Ithacans are and always have been great sailors and voyagers. When they come home it is by boat to Vathý.

The arrival at Vathý is, in a sense, a homecoming for all visitors, wherever they are from. As we sat in the limpid light of evening on the terrace outside the little house we had rented, which overlooked the haven, we could feel the spell of the Ithaca of the imagination. The mirror-calm water reflected houses and mountains: sea and land embraced each other. 'Ithaca is your predestination,' the Greek poet Constantine Cavafy tells his readers. Yet the message of the haven remains, like its celebrated hero, ambiguous and elusive: it spells both the longing for home and the longing for adventure. Return *and* departure.

It is an odd place for one of the great heroes of Homeric epic to come from. Just as it is today on the 'wrong' side of Greece for island-hopping, so it was on the wrong side to share in the great exploits of ancient times. To get to Troy (on the coast of present-day Turkey) in the first place, Odysseus would have had to sail round the Greek mainland before crossing the Aegean Sea. To return, he had to double Cape Maleia (Maléa), the perilous southeastern tip of the Peloponnese. That was where his nine years of wanderings began.

Our Odyssey took us to many places on the Greek mainland and islands, and to Turkey. But there were three key locations: Cape Maleia, the dividing point between reality and the imagination; wind-swept Troy, the isolated ruins of a once-great city; and Ithaca, the harbour of homecoming and departure.

The wake of the ferry as it departs from Vathý.

2 HOMER AND HIS AUDIENCE

When 'omer smote 'is blooming lyre,
'E'd 'eard men sing by land an' sea;
An' what 'e thought 'e might require,
'E went an' took – the same as me!

Rudyard Kipling

The suitors, all one hundred and eight of them, lie dead in bloody heaps, sprawled over the floor of Odysseus' great feasting-hall. Leodes, the man employed by the suitors to perform sacrifices for them, begs Odysseus for mercy; but he is rejected on the grounds that he must often, as part of his job, have prayed for Odysseus never to return. Odysseus chops off Leodes' head. Things do not look good for another man who is still left alive:

> Phemius singer of poems   used to play for the suitors,
> though not through free will.   He had avoided the dark void
> of death, and stood there   clutching his tuneful lyre,
> close by the side door.   His mind was divided
> whether to slink from the hall   and take asylum at the altar
> of Zeus of the house-yard,   where Odysseus used to sacrifice,
> or whether to throw himself   at the master's mercy.
> As he agonised,   it seemed the better strategy
> to cling round the knees   of Odysseus, Laertes' son.
> He laid down his hollow   lyre on the floor in between
> the bowl for blending wine   and the silver-studded seat.
> Darting forward   he clasped Odysseus' knees,
> and pleading for life   winged him these words:
> 'Mercy, Odysseus,   take pity and spare me.
> Later you'll feel   remorse if you slaughter
> the poet, a poet who   performs both for gods and men.
> My art is my own,   and the Muse has mapped in me
> complex paths of poetry.   I'm fitted to perform for you
> as for a god. So don't   cut my throat in your rage.
> And your own dear son   Telemachus may tell
> how, when I was in your house   to sing to the suitors
> after their feasting,   it wasn't by my wish or will.
> They were many and mighty   and forced me to perform.'
> He spoke, in earshot   of mighty Telemachus,
> who quickly came close   and said this to his father:
> 'Stop. Don't stab him   with a sword-thrust.
> He's innocent. . .'

Odysseus does spare Phemius. It is not only that he is not guilty: Odysseus needs a witness to his great deeds, a narrator who will tell of them and pass them down to future generations. The aim of life for the epic hero is immortal fame; and that means becoming the subject of song, of poetry. The hero needs the poet if his name is to survive, and Odysseus needs Phemius alive if he is ever to have his *Odyssey*.

HOMER. LIVE!

The *Odyssey* is in many ways about poets and poetry. Two bards are prominent within the poem: Phemius on Ithaca, and Demodocus among the Phaeacians on the island of Scherie. They deliver poems to please the banqueters in the palace, tales of apparently one or two hours' length. They perform to their own accompaniment on a plucked, stringed instrument, the *phorminx* or *cithara* (translated as 'lyre'). We might seem to have, then, a kind of autobiographical picture of Homer's own professional life. But there is a serious objection to this. The *Odyssey* cannot, we believe, have been originally or primarily created to be cut up into pieces of one or two hours' duration. No doubt shorter extracts could be performed on occasion, but in its entire artistic conception the work is like a huge integral tapestry, not a bag of patchwork pieces.

Perhaps the most widely known theory of all about the *Odyssey*'s authorship is that it was the work of a 'committee', that is to say, it can be broken down into component parts that may be attributed to several separate poets. But that theory is out-of-date. We strongly believe, on the contrary, that all or virtually all the poem was shaped by a single maker. One of our chief reasons for believing this is that, for all its many adventures and changes of scene, the *Odyssey* does *not* readily break into parts. Its flow and continuity defy division (the 24 books into which it is conventionally divided are merely a later editorial convenience). Within the *Odyssey* there is, we believe, only one fundamental breaking-point, the one between the poem's two very different yet subtly balancing halves.

The poem is all-embracing. It ranges over the known world and beyond, and yet it has a plain underlying shape. The key to the artistic construction of the *Odyssey* is that the voyages, spread over ten years, all come in the first half. It opens with Odysseus' son Telemachus' visit to Pylos and Sparta in the Peloponnese to seek news of his father. It then turns to Odysseus' own wanderings after he leaves Troy, which take him past Cape Maleia and over the seas to strange and magical places, even to the land of the dead at the very edge of the world. Halfway through the poem, Odysseus arrives back on Ithaca. The events of the second half take place within the span of only six days. Almost all are set on the small island, mostly within the single location of Odysseus' palace. The whole sequence of the contest of the bow and the slaughter of the suitors lasts a single day.

In terms of the number of verses, the division comes just over halfway through. Odysseus is on board ship on the very last stage of his voyage home:

They all leant to the oar   throwing spray with their blades,
while a sweet sleep   descended on his lids,
wonderful unwakeable,   next door to death. . . .

The ship slipped onwards   cutting through the water,
transporting that man   whose mind rivalled the gods,
who had borne before   all sorts of trials and troubles,
both in battles on land   and crossing the stressful sea.
But now he slept in peace,   forgetful of all past pain.

We hear in this echoes of the opening verses of the poem: 'that man
who . . . bore all sorts of troubles', in war and on the sea.
The second half of the poem then begins:

About the hour   when that brightest star rises
which shines to announce   the first flush of dawn,
the ship from over the sea   arrived at the island.
In the country of Ithaca   is the cove of Phorcys,
the ancient god of ocean.   There is a pair of promontories. . .

Everyone is used to reading stories divided into many chapters; and
the division of the *Odyssey* into 24 books (the work of scholars in
Alexandria long after Homer) seems very convenient. So why
should Homer have given his work only one organic stopping point?
A similar question arises with regard to the even longer *Iliad*, which
has (we believe) two organic divisions within it. We cannot tell without asking more about the people for whom these huge epic poems
were created and the circumstances in which they were delivered.
This is the Homeric Question, which has always been the subject of
hot and unresolved dispute amongst scholars.

If our theory about the poem's fundamental division into two parts
is right, then it seems to lead to the conclusion that the *Odyssey* was
created for performance, not reading. No one could be expected to
read the poem in two immense sections: it was made to be delivered
out loud in two live sessions.

At first sight, such long sessions might seem incredible. A specula-
tive but reasonable assumption about the speed of delivery suggests
that the first half could be sung in about ten and a half hours and the
second in nine and a half hours. But performances of this length are
not unknown in the world today. In the Soviet Republic of Uzbekis-
tan, for example, the performance of epic lasts from sunset to
sunrise, and continues for several nights, from three or four days to a
week or more. During that time the storyteller performs one or
several epics, depending on the tempo and his listeners' attention. In
Malaysia and Java the great Sanskrit epics of the *Mahabharata* and
Ramayana are enacted in shadow plays accompanied by a *gamelan*
orchestra; the performance begins after evening prayers and goes on
till dawn. It is not so easy to think of modern Western equivalents;
we seem to have neither the communal experience nor the patience.
The Royal Shakespeare Company's *Nicholas Nickleby* or the great
'Live Aid' concert at Wembley, offer only pale parallels.

A fifth-century Athenian vase-painting of a rhapsode, *a professional performer of epic poetry. Unlike the original poets he does not accompany his performance on a lyre.*

Phemius and Demodocus are not, then, self-portraits of Homer in performance. There is, however, one all-night feat of poetry described in the *Odyssey*, when the storyteller is Odysseus himself. As he tells his adventures to the Phaeacians, he eventually tires; but their king Alcinous insists:

> 'There is such charm   in your words and such wisdom;
> you have told your tale   as entrancingly as a poet,
> all your own painful   griefs, and the rest of the Argives'. . . .
>
> The night still stretches   ahead, and it's not yet time
> for sleep in this palace.   Tell us more of your story.
> I could stay awake   till dawn, if only you'd find
> it in you to tell   in this hall how you suffered.'

Odysseus rallies and continues through the night.

A FESTIVE OCCASION

It seems, then, unlikely that the *Odyssey* was created for a nobleman's entertainment, sung to order like the short lays of Phemius. What, in that case, would have been a suitable occasion, and who would have been the audience? During the eighth and seventh centuries BC – the time of Homer, who lived somewhere between 750 and 650 BC – popular festivals were beginning to spring up in Greece, held at the great religious centres, such as Delos and Delphi, sanctuaries of Apollo, which were becoming fully established at this time. People from a wide area would gather to celebrate, and the festivities would spread over several days. Many animals would be sacrificed, and much meat eaten and wine drunk. There would be competitive entertainments, especially athletics. The games at the great sanctuary of Zeus at Olympia in the Western Peloponnese, held every four years, claimed to be the oldest. They were traditionally said to have first been held in 776 BC.

The Ionians, the people of the part of Greece that Homer came from, held one such festival, the Panionion, at the sanctuary of the sea-god Poseidon near Miletus, and another on the island of Delos. A poet, perhaps a century and a half after Homer, tells of 'Delos where the long-robed Ionians congregate, along with their children and wives, to delight Apollo, whenever they hold the contest with boxing and dancing and poetry'. These festivals would have offered a good opportunity for a poet to capture a large audience in a receptive – and generous – mood. We think it most likely that the original performances of the *Odyssey* would have been at occasions such as these – at Delos, or perhaps even at the Olympic contests.

Imagine the occasion. As evening falls, after a day of festivities and athletics, men, women and children in their hundreds settle on the ground with blankets and cushions. The flames of their fires light their faces as they listen enraptured to the bard who picks up the pathway of his poem. On through the night, with occasional short breaks, they listen, without any inclination to fall asleep (except the children perhaps) until, towards dawn, with Odysseus sleeping his sleep next door to death, they settle down, soothed with storytelling and 'forgetful of all past pain'. Next evening the bard will continue.

'The public is the manure on the roots of all artistic activity,' according to Cesare Pavese, the modern Italian poet. Homer's publics are perpetual; but the Greeks at those great two-night sessions had the privilege of nurturing the first growth of this still-flourishing tree.

A generation or two before Homer, there would have been no occasion for such huge compositions as the *Iliad* and the *Odyssey*. His predecessors no doubt performed in feasting-halls to local lords and their retainers, and presumably their poems usually lasted one or two hours.

GOLD AND CLAY

So the huge scope of the *Odyssey* is a product of Homer's own day, and was created for an occasion that was a recent development in Greek life. Yet his poems are not stories of the everyday life of his own times. Far from it; they are set in a distant past, an age of heroes, of kings of great wealth and power, with mighty palaces and artefacts of gold. They dined on roast meat every day, not just on special occasions.

It is a nostalgic fantasy world, and yet it does have some connection with a reality. There really was an age of great wealth and power several centuries before Homer, during the period that archaeologists call the Late Bronze Age. Its uncovering, pioneered by the German enthusiast Heinrich Schliemann in the second half of the nineteenth century, followed later by more painstaking and scholarly excavators, is one of the greatest stories of archaeology.

The period in Greece from about 1600 to 1150 BC is known as the Mycenean Age, after the prosperous and powerful royal palace at Mycene in the northeastern Peloponnese, which dominated the fertile plain of Argos to the south and the route into northern Greece. There is no archaeological evidence to suggest that Mycene was dominant over other similar palaces throughout mainland Greece, such as those at Thebes or Pylos. It has, however, given its name to the culture that was centred on these citadels.

Certain physical reminders of this age, such as the magnificent Lion Gate at Mycene, remained visible down through the centuries into modern times, and the ancient Greeks must constantly have come upon vestiges of this past. Partly because of epic poetry, it re-

Some of the most beautiful artefacts of the great Mycenean Age are inlaid dagger blades. The scene on this one is reminiscent of some of the similes in the Iliad.

The Lion Gate at Mycene painted by Edward Dodwell (1821). It was cleared of debris by Schliemann in 1876.

mained for them (as for later generations) a legendary rather than historical time. It was not until the last part of the nineteenth century that this rich civilisation began to emerge as a historical reality. The gold masks and cups, the exquisite jewellery and inlaid daggers, the fine pottery and the monumental walls and buildings of the Mycenean Age that Schliemann and others uncovered are now familiar.

These people were outward-looking. The Mycenean artefacts found as far afield as Egypt and Syria in the east and Sicily and Corsica in the west are clear evidence of a great network of traders who ventured abroad, above all in search of precious metals. The mighty warlords needed gold for the ornaments that adorned them in life and in death, and bronze for the armour which they wore in battle. People used to think that the Myceneans were simply a warlike people, rather like the Vikings, who ruled the surrounding territory by sheer might. In 1953, however, the brilliant young architect Michael Ventris deciphered the symbols (known as Linear B) inscribed on a huge number of clay tablets that had been found at Knossos on Crete, and at Mycene and Pylos. The Linear B script turned out to be a form of Greek writing suited to clerical needs. It now became clear that each palace had been a centre of bureaucratic organisation. Inventories were kept, which recorded in detail taxes levied and the passage of every jar of oil and every sack of grain in and out of the gates.

*A typical Linear B tablet.
The script, which included
ideograms such as the chariot
wheels here, was scratched on
clay by professional
administrators.*

Although the world depicted in Homer's poems may have echoes of the great wars fought in bronze armour in the Mycenean Age, they retain no trace whatsoever of the social system that produced this bureaucracy or its elaborate writing. The whole sophisticated civilisation of the Mycenean world disappeared, for reasons that remain disputed and unclear, during the twelfth century BC. Mycene itself was sacked at least twice, and by the end of the century its society had totally disintegrated. Peasants may have squatted in the palace for a while, but the great citadel then became deserted.

THE AGE OF IRON

For 250 years, from about 1100 until about 850 BC, Greece was sunk in a Dark Age of poverty, depopulation and illiteracy. Overseas contact stopped; building, pottery, metalwork and all other artefacts regressed to a primitive level. To shed what little light we can on these times it is necessary to leave the splendours of Mycene and go to a place that, being less important, survived, though in much reduced circumstances.

Lefkandí, named after the nearby modern village, is situated on a west-facing headland on the long island of Euboea (Évia). Archaeologically it is the most important Dark Age site in Greece though, appropriately enough, all there is to see is a big hole in the ground. In the 1970s, British archaeologists, who were able to purchase only a small patch of land for excavation, sank a hole to bedrock in one corner of the site. This proved to go down through about 30 feet of ancient occupation levels. The hole is scarcely a tourist attraction – even the goats keep well away – but it has enabled archaeologists, by studying the stratification of the pottery found in these levels, to reconstruct the chronology of Greece from very early Mycenean times right through the Dark Ages and down to about 700 BC, when the town was deserted.

It seems that the people of Lefkandí during the Dark Age period were somewhat better off than their contemporaries elsewhere in Greece. It is impossible to tell what sort of social organisation they had, but there seems to have been a recovery in economic life and increasing contact with the outside world, which started slowly in about 950 BC, and then accelerated from 800 BC onwards. Some time in this period a new technology, iron smelting, was mastered: the Iron Age had arrived. Culturally, however, Greece seems to have been only gradually recovering from a coma. One art form alone presumably flourished. Isolated and poor, the people looked back to the great age of power and prosperity; and without the aid of writing, they had only one record: oral poetry.

The great 'hole' at Lefkandí, which now has a fig tree growing in it. Some stratification and remains of pots can still be seen in its strictly vertical sides.

The remains of a fine gateway in the monumental walls of classical Eretria. (The historian Dr Oswyn Murray is being interviewed down in the elaborate drainage channel.)

It must have been during these centuries that poems about the great heroes were being built up and passed on by bards. As poet taught poet, the picture of Mycenean times grew gradually further from historical reality and into an artefact in its own right. For oral poetry is not merely a memory device, it is also an art form, an art form that developed continuously until it reached its climax in the genius of Homer.

NEW HORIZONS

Homer himself does not belong in this age. Lefkandí was deserted, probably because of a war with the neighbouring city of Chalcis, between 750 and 700 BC. A new city, built some 10 miles further south at Eretria, replaced it. This typifies a society of Homer's day; and it clearly belongs to a different world. Founded on unsettled land in the plain beneath its fortified citadel, or acropolis, Eretria represented a fresh start for the people of Lefkandí, who could plan their new city with as much or as little regard for their old home as they chose. Created around the idea of a central open space, the houses, temples, streets, complex drainage system and city walls are built of huge blocks of finely cut masonry.

These were not the fortified homesteads of a few warlords with their retainers and serfs. Eretria was a city belonging to a community

34

of citizens, who fought in its army and participated in its institutions. It already had the makings of a city-state, the *polis* of classical times. In the following centuries Eretria developed all the characteristic features, including a gymnasium, a fine theatre and even a school of philosophy.

In its first years in the second half of the eighth century, Eretria participated as actively as any city in Greece in the newly expanding contact with the wider world, east, west and south. Close links were built with the trading-post at Al Mina in Syria, and a colony established on Ischia in the Bay of Naples. The Eretrians soon learned new skills from their foreign contacts; above all writing – but a new, far more flexible form than Linear B. For it is at this time that the Greek alphabet emerged, closely based on the Phoenician alphabet that merchants from the Greek mainland must have encountered at places like Al Mina. Adopted from the east, it rapidly reached its fully developed state. It was soon taken west, and there it was adapted by the Etruscans and then the Romans, to become the standard Western European form of writing, which you are reading at this moment.

The traders did more than merely exchange goods and ideas. Their reports of foreign lands created a mental map of the Mediterranean on which new settlements might be made. The Eretrians, perhaps influenced by their own experience of founding a new town, were the first Greeks to send out independent communities to new places. In Homer's day and the following generation, boundaries disappeared and horizons expanded. Throughout the mainland and islands the seventh century saw the emergence of the citizen as a political power, the development of different kinds of poetry, the painting of fine figured pottery, the first stirrings of philosophy and science – the phenomenon of classical Greece was getting under sail. In a nutshell, Greece had gone into a material and cultural trough between 1100 and 850 BC. The age of gold and heroes came before that; Homer and the creation of our *Odyssey* after.

THE AURAL AND ORAL POET

The *Odyssey* grew out of the occasion and audience of Homer's own day. It is, we believe, infused with the spirit of his age. He has often been seen as a retainer, guarding the last stronghold of the memories of the glorious Mycenean Age. A new, more stimulating perspective sees him as the artistic counterpart to the adventurers of his own place and time who were pioneering the trackways of the sea and of the mind.

At the same time, the *Odyssey* undeniably contains elements, fragments, derived from the Mycenean Age and from the Dark Ages in between. The explanation of how this could have come about is one of the great breakthroughs of twentieth-century Homeric scholarship. It has been demonstrated that Homer was an oral poet. Whether or not he could write himself, he learned how to be a poet by listening to other bards, and he learned it in order to perform out loud. So, no less importantly, Homer was an aural poet, a poet listened to by an audience. Alexander Pope, one of his greatest translators, sensed this when he said 'Homer makes us hearers' ('Virgil' he added, 'leaves us readers').

Kipling's lines (quoted at the beginning of the chapter) are apt, except that they imply that Homer stole from his predecessors. In fact, like his fellow bards, he inherited a huge repertoire of lines, phrases and techniques built up over many generations. These preserved features of Mycenean language and life that are substantiated by the Linear B tablets – the very fact, indeed, that Mycene was once 'golden'. Homer has a phrase, to take one good example, meaning 'silver-riveted sword'. This uses the old Linear B word for sword while referring to a technique of metalwork which was lost after the end of the Mycenean era. The reason why these bits of 'history' are embedded in the poem is not that Homer set out to be historically accurate: the aim of the creative artist is, rather, to be vivid and plausible.

The vast repertoire of oral poetry was constantly changing. It would add a phrase here, shed another there, introduce new cultural features – such as the replacement of burial customs by cremation – but preserve old ones elsewhere; for example, the exclusive use of bronze weapons long after the introduction of iron. The result was an amalgam of language, a fusing of various dialects, archaisms and modernisms, as well as features of the material world drawn from different times and places – with, no doubt, an added element of pure fantasy.

The oral tradition handed down stories as well as the means of telling stories. So Odysseus himself had probably been a favourite character for many generations, possibly even as far back as Mycenean times. In this sense, Homer himself is part of the 'reception' of even more ancient Odysseuses.

It is a strange confusion that has led many people to turn to history and archaeology for confirmation of the world Homer depicts. They feel that his poetry is so 'real' that he must be recording an actuality. Similarly, people have searched for the wood of the Ark on Mount Ararat. The Bible, however, claims in some sense to be history: Homer does not. 'The man, my Muse, tell of that man. . .' This is inspired poetry, and it does not belong in the non-fiction section of the catalogue.

The process by which the creative mind transforms reality into art, an underlying preoccupation of this book, is one of the great mysteries of human life. The raw materials – the realities of experience, of learning, of history – go into the transforming imagination, and they emerge from it shaped and fused into the finished work of art. So Homer's ingredients included all the inherited contents of the oral tradition as well as the informing spirit of his own day. In a similar way, James Joyce's creativity combined the preoccupations of his own time and place with all of his wide reading, and especially the *Odyssey*, to produce *Ulysses*.

HOMER'S HOME

Nothing is reliably known of Homer himself that can help us to answer these questions about the original circumstances in which the *Odyssey* was composed. No personal records survive. We cannot begin to write a biography like that of Joyce by Richard Ellmann.

Nearly everyone agrees that Homer lived somewhere between 750 and 650 BC. We ourselves regard the period 700 to 650 BC as the most likely date for the creation of the *Odyssey*. This places it somewhat later than the orthodox view; but, among other things, the poem seems to reflect the increased contact between Greece and Egypt, which came about during the reign of the Egyptian king Psammeticus I (663–610 BC).

Many cities claimed to be Homer's birthplace. As a seventeenth-century epigram put it:

Seven wealthy towns contend for Homer dead
Through which the living Homer begged his bread.

There were, however, especially strong traditions that linked him with Smyrna (Izmir) on the mainland of Asia Minor (modern western Turkey), and with Chios (Híos), a large and prosperous island lying just off the coast. Both were in the area known as Ionia. On Chios in classical times a guild of performers, or *rhapsodes*, called themselves 'the sons of Homer', *Homeridae*. They claimed to preserve their ancestor's work perfectly, down to the tiniest intonation.

Nobody knows for sure how and when the epics of Homer were first recorded in writing. In 700 or even 650 BC, the skill of writing had been so recently reintroduced into Greece that the sheer technology of it was still unwieldy. There is a strong tradition that an official text was made in Athens in about 530 BC. It may have been through the 'tape recording' recitations of the *Homeridae* that the poems had been preserved for the passage of a hundred and fifty years; or possibly they had been laboriously transcribed earlier.

Chian folklore places the *Homeridae* in the town of Volissos in the northwest of the island. It is named in the ancient, fictional biographies of Homer as the place where he spent his early career. Today it is a long drive over the bare mountains in the centre of the island to what is now a pleasant, though somewhat run-down, village on the hillside beneath a fine medieval castle built by the Genoese when their trading empire ruled the island. Near the top are the dilapidated ruins of an old house which has clearly been through many stages of rebuilding. A marble plaque records that this is, according to tradition, the house of Homer. Pure legend, of course; yet we were fascinated to find that the broken fragments of hundreds of ancient wine-jars had been built into the walls (a reminder that in ancient times, unlike today, Chios was famous for its wine). Rather as Homer retains fragments of a real Mycenean Age, but transformed through memory and storytelling, so this place retains the broken traces of the ancient world, transformed and made significant by the traditions of modern Greece.

THE GIFTED JOURNEYMAN

Even if Homer was based in Chios, as he may well have been, he would have had to travel to make his living and to find his audience. This will have taken him to the big religious festivals, which we have suggested were the original occasion for the *Odyssey* and the *Iliad*. Whether or not the work of the same Homer, both these great epics would have been developed over time, perhaps a whole lifetime. Year by year each would have been pruned and tended – a scene added here, a character discarded there – until, like an olive tree cultivated over many seasons, it reached a mature shape, unique yet impossible to improve.

There is one intriguing reference in the *Odyssey* to a travelling bard, as opposed to one attached to a palace, like Phemius and Demodocus. It comes in a list of visitors that a man might positively go out of his way to welcome:

> No one with any sense   goes out to bring in strangers,
> except for those experts   who help all of the people,
> such as seers, or healers,   or a craftsman skilled
> with wood – or with words,   the poet who spellbinds with song.
> These are the helpers   who are sought out everywhere.

So a bard is a kind of public servant, an individual with unusual gifts, who is sought out. No wonder, for he offers delightful entertainment. Odysseus says:

> It's good indeed   to sit and listen to a poet,
> one such as this, who has   a voice like a divinity.
> There's nothing I know   more completely pleasing
> than when contentment comes   upon all the people:
> the feasters sitting in   order throughout the hall
> pay attention to the poet;   beside them the tables are loaded
> with bread and roasted meat;   the bringer of bright wine
> dips into the big bowl   and pours out into cups.
> This, it seems to me,   is the finest time in life.

All these public servants – seers, doctors, carpenters – have something else in common: they bring order to the community, they shape raw material, and they clarify apparent confusion. The poet takes the chaos of life and makes some kind of sense and order out of it. This is, we think, still true of any poet worthy of welcome. As Odysseus says to Demodocus:

> Throughout the earth   and among all people, the poet
> should have his due share,   and be esteemed, as the Muse has
> taught him the paths of poetry,   loving the troop of true poets.

When Odysseus strings the bow as the prelude to restoring order to the chaos and injustice on Ithaca he is likened to a poet stringing his instrument. The resemblance goes deeper: he is himself a storyteller of great skill who can spellbind his audience. Getting on for a quarter of the *Odyssey* is recounted by Odysseus himself. He tells of the years that he spent between leaving Troy and arriving on Calypso's island. The account that he gives to the Phaeacians is over 2000 verses long, and would probably have taken more than three hours in performance. At the end:

> they sat in silence
> all through the twilit hall,   enthralled by the spell of his story.

Alcinous praises him for telling his story 'as entrancingly as a poet'.

Odysseus' versatility includes the art of poetry. Yet there is someone even more versatile than he is – the poet behind the poet. For it is not ultimately Odysseus who tells his story 'as entrancingly as a poet'; it is Homer. Homer is Phemius and Demodocus and Odysseus, the carpenter and the prophet and the doctor. He is the gifted journeyman who brings shape out of the chaotic raw material of human existence.

ABOVE LEFT] *The authors on their pilgrimage to Volissos.*

LEFT] *A wall of 'Homer's House' at Volissos on Chios. Many broken pieces of ancient wine amphorae are built into it.*

3 NEW WORLDS
FOR OLD

O my America, my new found land,
My Kingdom, safeliest when with one man manned,
My mine of precious stones, my empery,
How blest am I in this discovering thee!

John Donne, To his Mistress Going to Bed

The locations of the *Odyssey* are spread all over the known world –
and beyond. Like the powerful cameras on *Discovery* in *2001 A Space
Odyssey*, the poet can focus in on any particular spot he chooses.
When Homer pinpoints Odysseus for the first time in the poem, he is
sitting on the shore of an island staring disconsolately out to sea. His
back is turned on a demi-paradise, half-wild, half-artifice:

> A copious grove grew   around about the grotto,
> alder and tall poplar   and sweet-scented cypress;
> birds with swooping wings   had established their nests here,
> owls, hawks, falcons   and sharp-beaked sea-shags.
> A thriving vine   twined around the roomy mouth,
> burdened with grape bunches;   four founts closely clustered
> flowed in different directions   with crystal-clear water;
> lush pastures flourished   with wild parsley and violets.

There is only one other named inhabitant, and she is inside her
cavern-palace, working at her loom with a shuttle of gold and
singing, the nymph Calypso.

When Odysseus arrived here seven years earlier he was a shipwrecked sailor clinging to a plank, the last fragment of the fleet of
twelve ships he had taken to Troy. He had lost all his men and all the
spoils of war. 'For nine days he drifted,' as Tony Robinson tells the
story,

> his legs and toes began to wrinkle like a man who's fallen asleep in
> the bath. On the tenth morning he came to the island of Ogygia.
> He lay in the shallow water, too exhausted to drag himself up on to
> the beach, and looked up. Standing over him was the most
> stunning-looking young woman he'd ever seen. . . . 'I'm the
> nymph, Calypso,' she said, pulling him to his feet. 'I'm glad
> you've come to stay.'
>
> 'I haven't!' replied Odysseus. 'I'm the King of Ithaca, and I've
> got to get back to my wife and my son and my kingdom.' . . .

Odysseus thought about it. He looked at the little grass hut, at the palm trees full of bananas and coconuts, at Calypso's beautiful, lonely face.

'OK,' he said. 'I'll just come in for a quick coffee.'

Calypso looks after him and gives him the freedom of her bed, which at first he relishes. 'It was the longest cup of coffee ever.' But Calypso's name means in Greek 'concealer', and over the years Odysseus has been lost to the world while lying in her embrace. No one knows where he is; he is as good as dead, reduced to a memory, a name, a story. Odysseus has tired of the perfection of Calypso's body and of her island with its magical isolation. She provides an *embarras de richesses*, while he longs for humble humanity, for society and for his place in the world at large. If he stays with 'concealer' he will never merit his *Odyssey*.

Kingdom and fame are not all that Odysseus misses. Calypso offers him immortality as her bedfellow, but he longs for his mortal ageing wife. He says to her:

Don't be angry, goddess:
prudent Penelope   is less elegant and less

An olive tree on Ithaca with a trunk 'as thick as a pillar'. This may be as much as 1000 years old.

> beautiful than you – after all she's mortal
> while you're forever young.   All the same I always long
> and hope to make it home   to see the sun of my return.
> And if some god should shatter   my craft on the wine-like waters,
> I'll still endure it   with a patient spirit.
> Already I've endured   and stood the test of trials
> in wars and over waves.   So I'll confront one more.

The attraction of Penelope lies precisely in her mundane humanity. The poet Louis MacNeice brings this out in *Day of Returning*, which is set on Calypso's island:

> Behind him also, faintly curling out of the woods, a voice,
>   Which once entranced, now pained him; instead of that too
>   sweet song
> He yearned for the crisp commands of laundry and kitchen
>   Which his wife must be giving in Ithaca.
>
> For here his bed was too soft and the wine never rough and the
>   scent of the flowers
>   Too heavy; here when he should have smiled he wept;
>   . . . while a voice sang on, destroying
>   All heart, all hope, all Ithaca.

THE RAFT AND THE BED

The marital bed on Ithaca is the goal of the *Odyssey*. Odysseus achieves his long-awaited reunion with Penelope when at long last:

> they with a warm welcome   returned to their old bed.

Odysseus himself made that bed. Only he and Penelope and one maid knew its secret. When he describes how he made it, he takes a pride in the details of his craftsmanship – such labour is not beneath his dignity:

> In the yard there used to be   a thriving olive tree, leafy and
> full-grown   with a trunk as thick as a pillar.
> I built my bedroom   from scratch around that stock.
> I walled it in with blocks   and roofed it over fully,
> and added morticed doors   fitted neat to their frame.
> Only then I trimmed   the limbs of the leafy olive,
> and planing it with a blade   from the root to the top of the trunk,
> calling on all my skill,   I smoothed it true to a line;
> thus I crafted the corner post.   I bored holes with an augur,
> and working from here I framed   the bed from beginning to end.
> I inlaid the wood with gold   and white ivory and silver,
> and fitted leather thongs   across, dyed deep with purple.
> And that tree's the secret token   which I built into my bed.

The marriage bed is, then, literally rooted in the soil of Ithaca; and it is constructed around a trunk of the olive tree that vitally nourishes the people of the Mediterranean.

Number 7 Eccles Street,
Dublin (now demolished).

Number 7, Eccles Street, Dublin is the Ithaca of James Joyce's *Ulysses.* There Molly Bloom is first encountered half-asleep in the 'twilight' of her cavern-like bedroom. In Gibraltar, where she grew up, her first suitor was a young lieutenant on *HMS Calypso.* Now her husband Leopold Bloom, as he makes breakfast downstairs, hears and reflects upon '. . . a warm heavy sigh, softer, as she turned over and the loose brass quoits of the bedstead jingled. Must get those settled really. Pity. All the way from Gibraltar.' Above the bed hangs a picture entitled '*The Bath of The Nymphs*' (which came free with 'the Easter number of *Photo Bits*'). As Molly sips her tea, Bloom notices the resemblance between the captivating Nymph and his wife: 'Not unlike her with her hair down: slimmer. . . . She said it would look nice over the bed.'

Odysseus and Penelope did not have long to enjoy their bed in their prime. Their only child was still a baby in his mother's arms when his father was summoned to Troy. The cause of one unfaithful wife drew many thousands of young husbands away from Greece to Troy, and many of them never set off on the return journey. They were not concealed for seven years by Calypso, but for ever by the soil of Troy.

Calypso only lets Odysseus go because she is told to by the Olympian gods – they are persuaded that he has been obscured for long enough. She takes him to her bed for one last time and in the morning gives him an axe:

> When she had shown him the trees   the nymph Calypso went
> home.
>
> Odysseus made quick work   of cutting the tall timber;
> he felled twenty in all,   stripped them with axe,
> skilfully shaped the timbers   and smoothed them true to a line. . . .
>
> As broad across   as the base which is laid out
> by a skilled shipwright   for a cargo coaster,
> as broad as that Odysseus   constructed his raft. . . .
>
> He fixed in a main-mast   with boards fitted about it,
> and added a rudder   so he could steer straight.
> He fenced in the raft   all around with willow
> to keep out the wave-swell,   employing plenty of wood.
> Calypso, divine nymph,   carried out cloth
> to make him a main-sail,   and he fitted that out too,
> attaching the straps,   the ropes and equipment.
> Lastly he levered   the raft into the surf.
> It was the fourth day before he'd completed this task.
> So on the fifth Calypso   sent him on his sea-way.
> She bathed him, clothed him   with fragrant fabrics;
> she stowed two skins   one of red wine, one of water,
> and supplies in a sack,   including some sweet treats.
> Lastly she raised a breeze   balmy and harm-free.

The American folk-singer Suzanne Vega captures this moment in a song on her 1987 album, *Solitude Standing*. *Calypso* sees the story from a female perspective:

> Now today
> Come morning light
> He sails away
> After one last night
> I let him go.
> My name is Calypso
> My garden overflows
> Thick and wild and hidden
> Is the sweetness there that grows
> My hair it blows long

Suzanne Vega, a modern Calypso.

> As I sing into the wind
> I tell of nights
> When I could taste the salt on his skin
> Salt of the waves
> And of tears
> And though he pulled away
> I kept him here for years
> I let him go.

Odysseus is now entirely by himself, and will remain by himself on the high seas for nineteen days, as he crosses from the world of monsters and nymphs to the world of humans. Unlike his marriage bed on Ithaca, anchored by carpentry to *terra firma*, this craft keeps on moving, carrying him over the restless waves towards home.

NAKED LANDFALL

There was always a delicate balance of power between the Greek
gods on Mount Olympus. Generally they respected each other's
wishes, or frustrated them surreptitiously. One of the gods was
absent when Athena, who was Odysseus' special supporter, persuaded the Olympians to release him: Poseidon who rules the sea.
He is also the father of the one-eyed giant Cyclops, Polyphemus.
When, seven years before, Odysseus had used his cunning to blind
his single eye, Polyphemus had called upon Poseidon:

> Earth-shaper Poseidon   gloom-haired, hear me:
> if I'm surely your son   and you're fully my father,
> stop Troy-taker Odysseus   from ever arriving home.
> Or if it's fated for him   to reclaim his family,
> to reach his rich house   and his fatherland, then
> let it be late and hard,   with all his comrades dead,
> stowed on a ship not his,   to find havoc in his home.

So when Poseidon returns (after seventeen days visiting his wor-
shippers in Ethiopia), and finds Odysseus afloat on his domain, he
raises a great storm and easily smashes all that laborious carpentry:

> As a gust scatters   a great heap of grain-husks,
> dry and light they are lifted,   whirled around here and there,
> so the breaker scattered   the timbers . . .

Odysseus loses everything and even has to strip off the heavy
clothing given him by Calypso. With nothing left but his physical
strength, his quick wits and his will to survive, he swims. Poseidon
lets him be.

> Two days he drifted   and two nights over the waves. Often
> and often he thought   that his last hour was looming.
> But when the curly locks   of dawn spread the third day,
> the wind dropped and gave way   to calm. Then raised on a crest
> he caught a quick glance   – not distant – of land.
> As welcome as would be   the first signs of reviving life
> to a family whose father   has lain suffering in sickness,
> long wasting away,   and loathed death has hovered close,
> yet, welcome, the gods' will   at last slips him from sickness,
> so welcome the woods   and the land seemed to Odysseus.
> He swam with a will   to get his feet onto firm ground.

The father who is near to death, the signs of returning life: this simile
evokes the son and wife who are waiting on Ithaca. The image is mir-
rored near the end of the poem when Odysseus and Penelope finally
embrace on their reunion:

> He wept as he wrapped his arms   round the wise wife who fitted
> his heart. As welcome as would be   the glimpse of land as they
> swim
> to men whose boat has been   smashed and swamped by Poseidon –

some few by swimming   escape from the ocean surf
and reach dry ground,   a scurf of salt crusts their skin,
and to tread solid land   is welcome, escaping the worst,
so welcome to her was   her husband as she beheld him,
unable to unbind   her creamy arms from his neck.

Odysseus' endurance through his dangers is bonded with his restoration to his family. To persevere is to be made whole.

Even after he has sighted land Odysseus is battered and torn by the rocks, and is nearly drowned in the surf, before he comes ashore at the outflow of a river. By the time he feels the solid river-bed beneath him he is almost extinguished:

His arms fell limp,   his knees both buckled under him.
The brine had broken   his very spirit. His flesh was all swollen,
and salt water spurted   from his mouth and nose as he spewed;
with no breath left   and no voice, he lay in a faint
under a dreadful   weight of weariness. Until at last . . .
wading out of the water   he sank down among the reeds,
and kissed the grain-giving ground.

Even now, though, in his exhaustion he does not stop thinking; his mind is still active. Night is falling: it will be cold by the river and he will die of exposure. If he makes for the woods higher up, he might fall prey to a predator. He risks this, nonetheless, and has not gone far before he finds two thick bushes growing close together with a dry space deep inside them. Inside is a mass of old leaves, and the naked Odysseus burrows into them to keep alive through the night.

As on a remote farm   a man without neighbours nearby
will hide a glowing log   beneath a heap of black ash
to save the seed of fires   and not to fetch a new flame from
elsewhere, so Odysseus   hid himself beneath the leaves.

'The seed of fire'; the seed of life.

The night that Odysseus spends homeless and caked with salt beneath the leaves could hardly be further from the night that he will spend with Penelope a week later. But there is a link:

He scrambled beneath   two trees which grew together
from the same root-stock,   one wild olive and the other tended.
The strongest gusts   of wet winter couldn't penetrate there,
nor the brightest beam   of sunlight filter in,
nor could showers soak through,   so closely interleaved
were they together.   Under here Odysseus hid.

Scholars and botanists dispute whether the wild bush is a wild olive branching from the same root-stock, or some other species growing right by it. Either way, the cultivated bush is an olive. When Odysseus sleeps above the roots of olive in that wild bedchamber, he is finally on his way home.

The Nausicaa scene painted by Sir Edward Poynter (1836–1919): some of her maids wash clothes, while others play ball. If the figure on the left is Odysseus emerging from the bushes, then he wears more clothes than in Homer!

PRINCESS IN A NEW LAND

Odysseus is woken in the late morning by the cries of girls playing ball. Nausicaa, daughter of king Alcinous of the Phaeacians, has travelled by mule-cart some way with her maids to do the palace washing at this convenient place where the river runs into the sea. After so long away from the real world, Odysseus is not even sure that it is human voices that he hears:

> What kind of land, I wonder,   have I arrived at this time?
> I don't know whether they're wild,   violent and lawless,
> or hospitable hosts,   fair and god-fearing.
> A female kind of call   encircled me just then,
> as though from the nymphs   who keep the mountain peaks,
> the springs of rivers   and lush meadow-lands.
> Or could I be close   to human beings who speak
> my mortal language?   Well, I must test and see.'

The trouble is that he has none of the accoutrements of respectability: he is encrusted with salt and stark naked. He breaks off some foliage to achieve the effect that so amused James Joyce. 'He was the first gentleman in Europe. When he advanced naked to meet the young princess he hid from her maidenly eyes the parts that mattered of his brine-soaked barnacle-encrusted body.' The scene which follows is so delicately handled that it inspired Goethe to embark on a play with Odysseus and Nausicaa as exemplars of unspoilt humanity; and it led the nineteenth-century novelist and essayist Samuel Butler to claim that the *Odyssey* had an 'authoress', an idea that intrigued James Joyce and provided the inspiration for Robert Graves' novel *Homer's Daughter*.

Odysseus uses all his courtesy and diplomacy to win Nausicaa's goodwill. She is clearly a marriageable young woman:

To you may the gods grant   whatever's your dearest dream –
a husband and a household   and like-mindedness;
for there's nothing fairer   than when a man and a woman
share their family life   with minds that think alike;
this annoys their enemies   and gives pleasure to well-wishers.

Before long Nausicaa is talking coyly of Odysseus as a possible husband, and her father Alcinous quickly latches onto the same idea. Nausicaa would be a delightful bride, and Scherie, the island of the Phaeacians, would be an almost utopian place to settle in. It is fertile and peaceful and devoted to the good life:

Our delights are dancing,   meals, music, poems,
Cool laundered clothes,   hot baths and bedtimes

as Alcinous says.

After the very varied treatment that Odysseus has met with during his adventures, Scherie is clearly different. Not only do the Phaeacians treat strangers in a civilised manner, they live in a familiar kind of community and setting. Nausicaa describes her city as a walled peninsular site, which sounds similar to those on the coast of Asia Minor in Homer's own part of the world. Many details in her description could have applied to ancient Smyrna, which was often supposed to be Homer's birthplace:

Then the road arrives   at the town with a high wall round,
and a safe haven   on either side of the city.
Going in is a narrow   causeway with boats beached
on either roadside.   Each man has his shore-space.
The assembly meets there   near the temple of Poseidon,
and has seats constructed   with blocks of quarried rock.

This was also just the kind of site that Greek colonisers were searching for as they established new cities in fertile but defensible places all round Sicily and South Italy, the Black Sea and even North Africa. Following the establishment of trading posts in about 800 BC, there was a spate of planting new colonies, which developed rapidly during the next two centuries.

The past history of the Phaeacians also seems to reflect these migrations, which were so much a part of the world of Homer and his audience:

In former days the Phaeacians   used to be in broad Hypereia,
close by the Cyclopes,   a bullying breed of creatures,
who by brute strength   used to harry them ruthlessly.
Nausithous shepherded   a migration away from there,
settling in Scherie   far from bread-baking humankind.
He built bastions   round the town, then the houses,
positioned the temples   and allotted land.

A pensive Nausicaa (c. 1878) *by Frederick Leighton, the leading figure among the Victorian artists who drew on ancient Greece for their subjects.*

The Greek city on the island of Corcyra – more familiar as Corfu – was founded as part of the movement westward. It was an important

ABOVE] *Like Homer's Scherie, Corfu is an island of great fertility, where 'fig follows fig'.*

ABOVE RIGHT] *An old woman gathers olives that have fallen from the tall olive trees characteristic of Corfu.*

port of call *en route* for Italy and Sicily. Many people in both ancient and modern times have equated Corfu with Scherie. It is easy to see why. It is a few hours' voyage north of Ithaca, Odysseus' destination, and of all the isles of Greece, it is the greenest and lushest. Oranges, lemons and apricots flourish in the plains, while on the slopes the olive trees grow taller and thicker than anywhere else. Compared with the dry, barren mountains of most of Greece, Corfu is a horticulturist's paradise – like the orchard and kitchen-garden of king Alcinous:

> This fruit neither fails   nor perishes, it is perennial
> winter and summer.   In the breeze of the zephyr
> some fruits forever   swell while others soften.
> Pear ripens on pear,   apple on apple, grapes
> bunch upon bunch,   while fig follows fig.
> Also in there a vineyard   full of fruit is rooted:
> a level space bakes   in the sun, where some bunches
> are harvested,   while others get trodden;
> in front are some in flower,   while others begin to blacken.
> Below the bottom row   grow neat beds of greens
> of various sorts, all   fresh throughout four seasons.

50

The modern Corfiots like the idea that their island is that of the Phaeacians. The favourite site for the palace of Alcinous is at Paleo-kastritsa on the northwest coast, where there is a picturesque peninsula with a harbour on either side. Some miles further north, at Agios Georgios Bay – rather a long mule-cart ride – a stream runs into the sea, and local legend identifies this with the place where Nausicaa did her washing. When we asked a local lad if the women still did their washing there, he told us that they all have washing machines now (though he admitted that his mother refuses to use hers, preferring her old wooden trough!).

The rock off Paleokastritsa on Corfu, which is popularly identified with the Phaeacian ship turned to stone in the Odyssey *by the god Poseidon in retribution for taking Odysseus home.*

Lechaion, the harbour of ancient Corinth for those departing west along the Gulf (with modern Corinth in the background). The 'hills' in the foreground and on the other side of the river are in fact the accumulations of many centuries of dredging.

VOYAGERS TO THE NEW WORLDS

The men and women who planted the Greek city on Corfu in 734 BC came from Corinth. Corinth, situated at the south end of the isthmus that separates the Peloponnese from the rest of Greece, is at the crossroads of Greece: the north–south axis is by land, and the east–west by sea. The city was perfectly placed to be receptive to new experiences and ideas, to absorb and develop them. A cultural melting-pot, Corinth invented a new 'orientalising' style of Greek art; its myths were imbued with the influence of the east, as were its cults – the famous temple of Aphrodite was the only one in Greece where, already in Homer's day, there was ritual prostitution.

Ancient Corinth had two harbours. From Kenchreai, which faces the Aegean, merchants and colonists set out for the Dardanelles, the Bosphorus and the Black Sea. From Lechaion on the Gulf of Corinth they embarked for Corfu, Sicily, South Italy and beyond. Lechaion is at a river-mouth, and repeated dredging over many centuries in ancient times built up two great hills on either side. The harbour itself silted up long ago, and now unexpected stretches of ancient harbour-walls stick up out of the mud and reed-beds, where birds and frogs live undisturbed. Yet, for all its air of desolation, Lechaion still retains an atmosphere, a trace of the hopes and fears of those who once set out from it.

After making offerings to Apollo at Delphi, only just out of sight across the Gulf, the colonisers would sail for their New World. Few would ever return. Under the leadership of one of their aristocrats, they would place the sacred flame from their mother city in a new shrine, and then set about organising their new city as a fully-fledged *polis* (like Eretria), but far away from the familiar world they knew.

They built walls and houses, made new temples for their gods, and allotted land.

The colonisers went for as many reasons as the early settlers went to America. Some were in official groups, some went out of a spirit of adventure, and because they hoped to make their fortunes and a better life. Others were driven out by political or religious persecution. Ancient documents from Cyrene (now in Libya) show that some settlers even went under compulsion. The people of the island of Thera passed a law that one member of each family should be sent on an expedition to the coast of North Africa – 'brother from brother', the inscription ominously reads. The death penalty was decreed for anyone who refused to go or who helped someone else avoid going.

When the colonisers reached Africa they were too afraid to land, and for a while they sat on a little island off the coast. When they tried to go home, they were prevented from even disembarking on Thera, despite the original agreement that, if the colony failed after a serious attempt, they could return home in five years time. They sailed back and eventually founded Cyrene, which became one of the richest cities of the Mediterranean. So much so, in fact, that several centuries later, the people of Thera had to draw the attention of the Cyrenians to another clause in the document, allowing Therans to come and settle at a later date in their colony.

The Phaeacians too became prosperous and happily settled in their new home. But it's no good pretending that Corfu is Homer's Scherie. Nausicaa's Stream, when we went there, was nearly stagnant and echoed not to the voices of girls but of frogs. It did not

'Nausicaa's Stream' at Agios Georgios Bay on Corfu, not even running out over the sands after the dry winter of 1988–9.

The double headlands at the popular tourist resort of Paleokastritsa on Corfu, not really like Homer's description of the city of the Phaeacians.

even reach the sea but ran into the sand at the top of the popular bathing beach. This disappointment can be attributed to the severe lack of rainfall in the winter of 1988–9; but the golden sands cannot. Homer makes it quite clear that the river where Odysseus lands issued from a rough and rocky coastline. At Paleokastritsa, furthermore, there is not one headland but two, thus making a triple harbour – a more striking feature, in fact, than Homer's setting. More seriously, however romantic the spot, archaeologists have failed to uncover any ancient remains at Paleokastritsa, whether from Mycenean times or Homer's.

The realities of Homer's own day have contributed to his account of Scherie, not in the topographical details of a particular place, but in spirit, in the sense of adventure and of a broadening of social and geographical horizons that it represents. In a rather similar way sailors' reports and pamphlets about the Bermudas entered Shakespeare's imagination when he created Prospero's island in *The Tempest*. In any case Homer, like Shakespeare, makes it quite clear that his island is *not* a real place. Alcinous' orchard is too prolific to be true, even on Corfu. His palace is guarded by magic watchdogs made of silver and gold. Scherie is outside the known world. As Nausicaa says:

We live on the furthest fringe   far apart in the turbulent
ocean; so other races   never come mixing with us.

54

Their boats do not need navigating and are invisible to strangers. It is true that it takes only one night to travel to Ithaca, but the boat travels supernaturally, 'faster than a falcon'. No one in Homer's real world had ever met a Phaeacian.

EXPLORATION VERSUS NOSTALGIA

Homer's Greece in, say, 700 or 675 BC was an exciting place. Colonisation and the opening up of new worlds was only one aspect of the rapid expansion taking place in politics, ethics, poetry and art. The spirit of discovery and innovation pervaded all of life, and fired the imagination, just as the opening up of America in the seventeenth century inspired John Donne's passionate declaration to his mistress.

The sense of exploration in the *Odyssey*, the sense of curiosity and the discovery of new places and ways of life, are a product of this age of colonisation. At the same time, it is easy to forget that Odysseus does not want to go on endlessly exploring; the compulsion comes on the whole from outside, especially from the anger of Poseidon, and not from within. Although Scherie is the right place for Odysseus to take stock – a sort of transition between the wild and the domestic olive – he is not tempted to stay in that delightful new world with its desirable princess. He wants to go home, back to rocky, unmagical Ithaca – in his own unapologetic words:

Rugged and bare it may be   but it breeds good children.

Homer creatively merges the ancient and the modern. The figure of Odysseus went back through centuries of the oral tradition of epic; but in the Scherie episode he is put into a setting drawn from the world of the poet and his audience. Adaptable as ever, he fits in easily. He is an appropriate hero, a prototype for such an age – an adventurous voyager, yet one who ultimately comes home.

There is a conflict within Odysseus and within the *Odyssey* between the desire for novelty and exploration and the desire for the reassuringly familiar and secure. Homer's own times knew apprehension and homesickness as well as excitement. This very combination of contradictions, the outward-bound spirit and the love of home, was to characterise the great Classical age of Greece. This was driven by the spirit of enquiry and of progress, but at the same time had a strong sense of 'safe-mindedness', that is of the dangers of excess and arrogance. That same combination of excitement and apprehension is characteristic, it seems to us, of the late twentieth century. It is one reason why Odysseus survives.

MONTES IDÆ

4

G

3

2

1

6

F

3

7

E

SCAMANDER Fl.

SIMOIS. Fl.

A

D

C

Rhœteum

B

Sigeum

A

A

MARE ÆGEUM

Ostia Scamandri

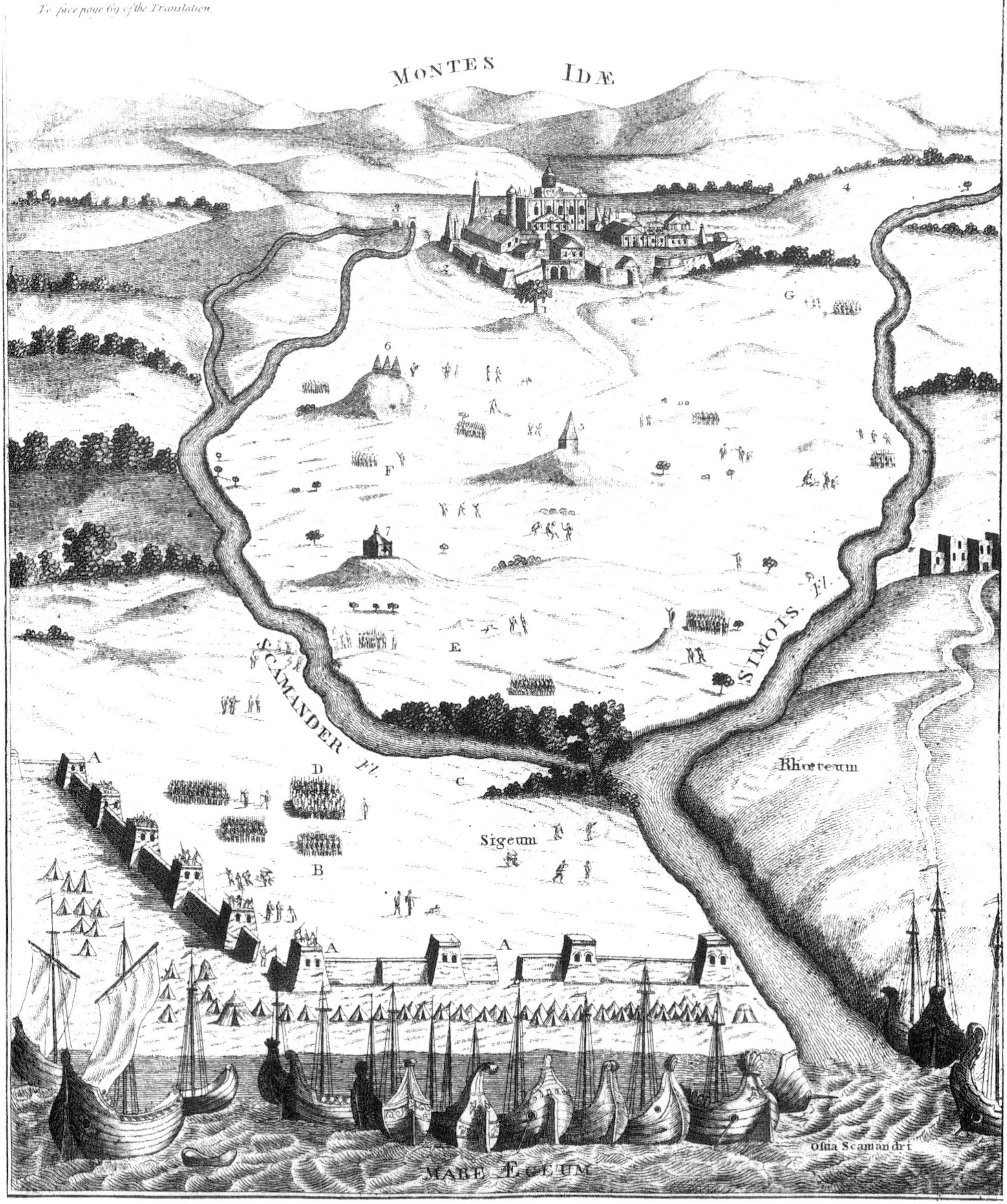

4 THE SPRINGS OF TROY

Know the context – pay attention to the circumstances of a work, the nature of the times, the manners, the landscape, the climate. Good art has its roots in a particular time and place. It may soar up to universality, but it is rooted in real life, it has the sap of particular people in it, it enjoys the sunlight of a particular sky.

David Constantine, Early Greek Travellers and the Hellenic Ideal
(on Robert Wood's attitude to locality)

While Odysseus is among the Phaeacians, the bard Demodocus sings three poems, each differently relevant to the as yet unnamed visitor. First, in the morning:

Once they had satisfied   the desire for food and drink,
the Muse moved the poet   to tell of the feats of heroes,
picking up the track of poetry   at a celebrated height:
the dispute when Odysseus   and Achilles, Peleus' son, clashed;
how at a holy festival   these two once wrangled with words. . .

This quarrel is not in fact celebrated anywhere else in the stories of Troy. So why should Homer choose to allude to it here?

The *Iliad*, the great epic of the 'feats of heroes', begins with a furious clash of words between Agamemnon, commander of the Greek army that went to Troy, and Achilles, Peleus' son. The phrase Demodocus uses here looks like a direct allusion to the first line of the *Iliad*:

Fury, the fatal fury of   Achilles, Peleus' son, inspire
that poem, my Muse. . .

Scholars still divide over whether the *Iliad* and the *Odyssey* are by the same poet. We are inclined to believe that they are by a single genius, different yet related, rather in the same way that Shakespeare's mature tragedies are related to his late plays. Either way, what is emerging more and more clearly from recent studies is that the *Odyssey* presupposes the *Iliad*, and that an audience that knew the poem of war and tragedy would appreciate the poem of peace and poetic justice more richly. So here Demodocus' topic reminds the audience, without spelling it out, that Odysseus was a prominent character in the *Iliad* and underwent its agonies:

An imaginary reconstruction of Troy and its landscape, based entirely on Homer, to accompany Alexander Pope's translation of 1720.

Fury, the fatal fury of   Achilles, Peleus' son, inspire
that poem, my Muse.   It massed agony on the Achaeans
and sent squads   of heroes' souls hurtling to Hades,
their corpses left as carrion   for dogs and flocks
of squabbling birds.   So Zeus' plan was completed.

Yet Homer or whoever gave the poem the title *Iliad* (or rather *Ilias*) – from Ilios, the usual Greek name for Troy, appreciated that while the poem is much concerned with the sufferings of Achilles, Odysseus and the other Achaeans (as Homer calls the Greeks), it is also profoundly sympathetic towards the Trojans, portraying Troy as a fine, civilised city, in no way barbarian or alien. It ends with the burial of the Trojan hero Hector.

The two finest things in the *Iliad* are both doomed. Achilles' life is intensified by the imminence of his death; and Troy's splendour is lit by the flames of its sack. Although these two events happen after the end of the poem, they are so vividly foreshadowed that it is as if they came within it.

TROY IN FLAMES

Hector is the greatest protector of Troy. He is killed by Achilles towards the end of the *Iliad*; but it is still quite near the beginning of the poem that we last see him with his wife Andromache. She pleads with him not to go back to the battlefield, but he insists that his honour demands it. He must win glory while he can:

For I know this full well   at the root of my heart and spirit:
the day will dawn   when Troy shall be destroyed
and Priam himself   and the people of Priam also.
Yet what hurts me most   isn't the future fate
of the wretched Trojans   or Hecuba or king Priam,
not so much my own   brothers who are bound to die
at enemy hands,   for all their worth and numbers:
none of this hurts so much as   the thought of you taken in tears
by some armoured Achaean   to forfeit the light of freedom.
You'll go to Greece to serve   the loom of an alien lady,
and to fetch water from   the springs of Messeis
or Hypereia – you'll have to,   whether you want to or not.
And someone seeing you weeping   may make the remark:
'That woman was wife to Hector,   the bravest and best
of the horse-taming Trojans   when they fought about Troy.'
So someone may speak,   and it will replenish your pain
to be widowed of the one   who used to keep capture at bay.
But I trust that the tomb   will hide my body under,
before ever I hear   the cry of your capture and rape.

The sack of the city would mean death for the men and slavery for the women. Andromache would be taken away to wait upon the wife of an alien lord, and to serve his bed if he so chose. The spring of Messeis was in Menelaus' kingdom, Hypereia in Achilles'.

The equivalent springs for Troy, essential to the city's health and fertility, are the source of the river Scamander (today, the Menderes). It is a symbolic moment in the *Iliad* when the fire-god Hephaestus burns Scamander into surrender, and the river-god has to promise Hera (who hates Troy):

> . . . I swear you to this oath: I shan't fend off the day
> of destruction from the Trojans,   not even when their homes blaze
> engulfed in flames,   the night the Achaeans set light.

Not long after this, Hector, the great defender of the city, is isolated outside the gates with Achilles rapidly approaching. His old father Priam pleads with him:

> My son, come inside   the walls to be the salvation
> of the men and women of Troy.   Don't allow Achilles
> the chance of great glory,   and so lose your life.
> Last but not least pity me   still conscious in my misery.
> Zeus will no doubt destroy me   on the threshold of old age
> with a hard death   after seeing atrocities –
> my sons slaughtered,   my daughters dragged off,
> their bedrooms ransacked,   and the little children
> broken on the rocks   in the wastefulness of war.
> And I last of all –   my own dogs will rend me raw
> before my own doorway,   after someone has ended my days
> with a thrust or blow of bronze –   the hounds I reared in my house
> to guard gate or attend table,   drunk to madness
> on my blood, they'll lie down   in front of my gate.

It is all too clear that Hector's death will spell the sack of Troy. Yet he stays outside to face Achilles, and he takes his final stand at a significant place, beside

> . . . the springs,   the flowing fountains,
> where well up the twin   sources of swirling Scamander.
> One runs with warm water   and steam rises from its surface,
> as smoke from a fire;   the other flows cold all through
> summer, cold as snow   or ice frozen by frost.
> Alongside these springs   are the spacious washing-places,
> finely formed of stone, where the wives of the Trojans
> and their daughters used   to wash the clothes till they shone,
> back in peace before   the Achaeans arrived at Troy.

The springs of the river, which has been so recently burned into surrender, stand here for Troy's past in peacetime, evoking the elemental delights of hot water in winter and the cool of the fountain in summer. When Hector dies, and Troy falls, the women will soon be working as slaves at foreign fountains, and their fine clothes burned or looted.

When Hector's body is being dragged along behind the triumphant chariot of Achilles, a cry of grief goes up in Troy. Homer produces an ominous comparison:

It was through and through   as though all tall Troy
were ablaze in flames   from bastion to base.

THE BURIAL OF HECTOR

The city of Troy was well built. Homer describes the great palace of
Priam, with its chambers to house his fifty sons and twelve
daughters with their wives and husbands. Hector, the best of his
sons, has his own palace where he lives with Andromache and their
baby son. During his final battle with Achilles, Andromache is
indoors weaving, as Hector would wish her to be:

Deep inside the high house   she was working at weaving
a purple double robe   with flower patterns picked out.
She commanded her housemaids   to prepare a tripod,
a great cauldron of hot water,   over the fire to provide
Hector with a hot bath,   when he returned from battle.
She little suspected, poor soul,   that all too far from baths
the glinting-eyed goddess Athena   and Achilles had killed him.

This passage particularly moved Simone Weil, the French intellectual, mystic and socialist, as the Germans advanced on her
country in 1939 (she was Jewish, and died in England in 1943).
'Indeed he was far from hot baths, this sufferer,' she wrote, 'nearly
all the *Iliad* takes place far from hot baths. Nearly all of human life has
passed far from hot baths.'
Andromache laments for her beloved husband:

Now by the ships with curved prows,   far apart from your parents,
the wriggling worms will consume,   once the dogs have done,
your corpse, naked,   yet in your halls lie clothes
of delicate texture,   fine handiwork of women.
I shall set them all   alight in blazing flames –
no use to you now   since you shall never be shrouded.

She is wrong, however. The *Iliad* ends not on a note of cruelty and
separation, but with a fragile scene of insight and sympathy. Priam
brings the ransom for the body of his son Hector to the tent of
Achilles, and Achilles accepts it. Out of the ransom, Achilles leaves
'two cloaks and a closely woven tunic' and wraps the body of Hector
in them. The poem concludes with the Trojans' burial of the ashes of
their prince, their only hope, after cremation on a pyre:

They gathered his ashes   and, wrapped in the purple
of a soft cloth, put them   inside a casket of gold.
This they lowered within   a hollow burial chamber,
and covered it over   with great shaped stones.
In haste they raised the barrow,   with guards posted round on
lookout in case the Achaeans   might mount an attack too soon.
After building the barrow   duly they gathered together,
and held a dinner of honour   in the palace of lord Priam.
Thus they finished the funeral   of horse-breaker Hector.

View towards Troy from the north. Hisarlık is in fact the foothill in the middle distance in the centre of the view.

Early on in the *Iliad*, at the end of the first day of battle, Hector issues a challenge to single combat. Honourable burial for the loser is part of his conditions; and he undertakes that, if he wins, he will take his victim's armour but:

> I'll give back his body   so the Achaeans can cover him
> and build him a barrow   by the broad Hellespont,
> so someone may say,   of the men of later times,
> as he sails his ship   across the wine-like ocean:
> 'That is the burial-barrow   of a man laid low in the old days;
> hero though he was,   great Hector killed him.'
> Such words will he say,   and my fame will live for ever.

RIGHT] *In this painting in the centre of a cup by Douris (Athens, early fifth century* BC), *Odysseus pleads with Achilles to stop sulking and to rejoin the war.*

BELOW] *Jean Auguste Dominique Ingres' first important work, painted in 1801 when he was 21, shows the representatives of Agamemnon coming to Achilles, as in the* Iliad. *Odysseus leads the three ambassadors.*

The poem ends, however, not with his opponent's burial-mound by the Hellespont, but with his own. Nonetheless, Hector wins the ultimate confirmation for the hero in epic, *Iliad* and *Odyssey* alike: immortal glory.

THE SURVIVOR IN THE MIDDLE

Hector and Achilles span the *Iliad*: the final verse is about Hector as the first is about Achilles. The contrasting archetype to Achilles among the Achaeans is Odysseus. But, although Demodocus recounts their quarrel, there is no direct antagonism between the two in the *Iliad*. On the contrary, Odysseus is one of the three special friends of Achilles who are chosen to plead with him to return to the field after he has quarrelled with Agamemnon, and to help the Achaeans in their trouble. Yet in that very scene the fundamental contrast between them emerges most clearly. Odysseus' speech to Achilles is a masterpiece of rhetoric, putting Agamemnon's offer of recompense in the best possible light and diplomatically suppressing words of provocative challenge. Achilles' reply, which is a total refusal, begins:

> Laertes' only son   ingenious Odysseus,
> I must talk straight   and say my bit bluntly,
> the way that I think,   and the way it will be,
> so you don't come to coo   beside me one by one.
> For as deadly hateful to me   as the gates of Hades is
> the man who mouths one thing   when another hides in his heart.

Achilles uncompromisingly speaks his mind, however much trouble that may bring: Odysseus on the contrary is the past-master at saying one thing and hiding another in his heart.

Odysseus and Achilles come into open disagreement later in the poem. Achilles has decided that he will return to the battle to revenge his companion Patroclus, and he is all for taking the field first thing in the morning even without any sustenance. Odysseus resists him politely but firmly: Achilles may be able to do without, but the rest of the army needs its breakfast:

> Peleus' son, and far strongest   of the Achaeans, Achilles,
> you are mightier than me   and far stronger in the field,
> but I might be your better   in thinking issues through.
> I am, after all, older   and have learned more lessons;
> so steel yourself   to listen to my lecture. . .
> It's no use the Achaeans   mourning a stiff with their stomachs.
> Too many tight-packed   fall down day after day –
> When would one ever have   a break from bemoaning?
> What we need to do is   to dig the dead under,
> and harden the heart   after twelve hours of tears.
> Those surviving   the horrible toil of battle,
> must think of drink   and of food, so as to fight
> relentlessly against   the enemy's men.

Despite the stories of his initial reluctance to go to Troy, once there Odysseus was, as James Joyce put it, a 'jusqu'auboutist'. He is a strong cohesive force among the Achaeans, and more than once in the *Iliad* he has to repair the damage done by Agamemnon. Early on in the poem Agamemnon badly misjudges morale with a speech in which he pretends to encourage everyone to pack up and go home. Before he can stop them they are busy launching the ships that have been beached for nine years; and it is Odysseus who has to take Agamemnon's sceptre from him and go around restoring order. He has a firm but polite speech for the leaders; but:

> If he came on any commoner   and found him still shouting,
> he would whip him with the   sceptre and sting him with
> > reproaches:
> 'Sit down, stay still,   and listen to what others tell you,
> obey your betters.   You are useless, yellow,
> not of any account   in battle or in debate.
> We Achaeans here   can't all be commanders.
> Many-generalship   is no good, one general will do well,
> let one lord lead,   the one chosen by Zeus.'

When they are reassembled, there is still one voice complaining, the ugly and cowardly Thersites, who has a biting satirical tongue. Thersites attacks Agamemnon in much the same vein as Achilles did in their great initial quarrel. But Odysseus can cope with a Thersites:

> 'Let me tell you this,   and this is how it will happen:
> if I find you again   fooling in this fashion,
> let this head rest no longer   on Odysseus' shoulders,
> let me be called the father   of Telemachus no more,
> if I don't go and   strip you to the skin,
> jerkin and cloak and all,   exposing your private parts,
> and chase you away   down to the hulks howling,
> beating you from our meeting   with the lash of humiliation.'
> So he spoke, and with the sceptre   whacked his back and
> > shoulders.
> He doubled up, and tears   filled his eyes, as a weal
> of blood blossomed   on his back from the blow
> of the gold-studded sceptre.   He sat down terrified,
> and looking lost   wiped the drops of his weeping.
> The men, annoyed though they were,   laughed gleefully at him,
> and one would say to another   turning to his neighbour:
> 'Odysseus has done   thousands of good things,
> giving us good leads   in debate and in battle;
> but this is the best blow   he has ever delivered,
> shutting this insulting   loud-mouth out from the meeting.'

Most Homeric warriors have their eyes on the past, but Odysseus has his on the future. The others often use their patronymic – Achilles is 'son of Peleus' and so on. Odysseus is the only one who identifies himself by his son as 'father of Telemachus'. This seems a

ABOVE] *Looking west towards the mouth of the Dardanelles. Troy is several miles inland on the left shore.*
BELOW] *The largest pool of the 'Forty Eyes', the springs at Pınarbaşı near Troy.*

ABOVE] *The monumental walls of the acropolis of Troy VI seen from the landward side.*
BELOW RIGHT] *The Roman city of Troy lies less than a metre beneath cornfields outside the acropolis of Troy.*

ABOVE] *The outlet of the most copious of the springs of Pınarbaşı.*

PREVIOUS PAGES] *Adam Elsheimer's evocation of the sack of Troy (c. 1600). Aeneas and his family make their escape.*

ABOVE] *Mycene with the plain of Argos behind. The Lion Gate is at the other side of the acropolis.*
BELOW] *The village of Volissos on Chios, where Homer is said to have lived.*

ABOVE] *Odysseus confronts Nausicaa with only a branch to cover 'the parts that matter', by Rubens.*
BELOW] *A voluptuous Edwardian vision of the Sirens by Herbert Draper (1909).*

LEFT] *In Turner's splendid painting (1829) Odysseus derides Polyphemus (detail).*

ABOVE] *A watercolour of Corfu by Edward Lear. He noted that it was painted at 4.30 pm on 24 February 1863.*
BELOW] *In the olive groves of Corfu, May 1989.*

ABOVE] *The haven of Vathý in the heart of Ithaca.*
BELOW] *Velanidhia, the last village before Cape Maleia, built on the hillside as a safeguard against piracy.*

ABOVE] *John Linnell (1792–1882) closely follows Homer's version of the landing of Odysseus on Ithaca.*
PREVIOUS PAGES] *The exotic charms of Calypso and her island
painted by Jan Brueghel the Elder and Hendrick de Clerck (c. 1600).*

ABOVE] *Arnold Böcklin stresses the estrangement of Odysseus and Calypso (1883).*
BELOW] *Fuseli responded to the pathos of the story of Polyphemus' blinding (1802).*

ABOVE] *The slopes between Marmarospilia and the Gulf of Ithaca.*

ABOVE] *A pastoral scene on Ithaca today.*
BELOW] *Ithacan pigs reminiscent of Eumaeus' farm.*

ABOVE] *Vathý reflected.*

ABOVE] *Penelope at her loom, by Pintoricchio (c. 1500). Odysseus as a beggar is in the doorway.*
BELOW] *A happy ending? Primaticcio's enigmatic reunion (c. 1563).*

clear indication that the poet of the *Iliad* was aware of the *Odyssey*.

In this scene Odysseus not only unites the army, but is also the mouthpiece of authority. In the *Iliad* as a whole, authority is questioned, especially by Achilles. Odysseus speaks out for order, and his contribution here has been much cited down the centuries by authors seeking antique precedent for their views. Sir Thomas Elyot in 1531, for instance, quoted him to show 'that one soveraigne governor ought to be in a publicke weale: and what damage hath happened where a multitude hath had equal authorite without any soverayne.' His book *The Governour*, dedicated to Henry VIII, won him the ambassadorship to the court of Charles V of France.

The best-known refashioning of Odysseus' argument in support of authority comes in Shakespeare's *Troilus and Cressida*, in the speech on degree. This epitomises the whole Elizabethan view of order. (Chapman's famous translation *Seaven Bookes of the Iliades* – later immortalised by Keats' sonnet, *On first looking into Chapman's Homer* – had been published in 1598.)

> The heavens themselves the planets and this centre
> Observe degree, priority and place,
> Insisture, course, proportion, season, form,
> Office, and custom, in all line of order . . .
> . . . Oh when degree is shak'd
> Which is the ladder to all high designs,
> The enterprise is sick. How could communities,
> Degrees in schools, and brotherhoods in cities,
> Peaceful commerce from dividable shores,
> The Primogenitive and due of birth,
> Prerogative of age, crowns, sceptres, laurels,
> But by degree stand in authentic place?
> Take but degree away, untune that string,
> And hark! What discord follows. . .

The Odysseus who is a pillar of the establishment nonetheless looks after Number One. The father of Telemachus intends to get home to his son. He is quite prepared to run rather than face suicidal odds in battle. At one point Diomedes calls on him to help him and old Nestor, but

> Enduring Odysseus   turned a deaf ear to his words.

THE MOUNDS BY THE HELLESPONT

As well as clearly envisaging the city of Troy and the surrounding landscape, Homer builds up a precise picture of the ships of the Achaeans which were pulled up on the beach nine years earlier. Huts have been built by them, and the relative positions of each of the commanders are clearly fixed. The place where Odysseus' boats were beached on the day of arrival at Troy epitomises his character. At one point Zeus sends Strife down to the ships:

Peter Jeffrey as Ulysses in the 1985 Royal Shakespeare Company's production of Troilus and Cressida.

> She took her stand   by the big dark ship of Odysseus,
> plumb in the middle,   where her loud shout might reach
> both wings. At one end   stood the tents of great Ajax,
> at the other those   of Achilles – fully trusting
> in their strength, these two   had beached their boats at the edges.

It is no coincidence that neither of these uncompromising individualists survives the war to return home.

Achilles' mother Thetis is a goddess, and, through a prophecy she has given him, he alone of the heroes of Troy knows his destiny for sure:

> If I hold on here   fighting the battle for Troy,
> my return home is nought,   but I'll get immortal glory:
> if I escape back there   to the land and fields of my fathers,
> my fine glory is nought,   but I'll secure long life.

Achilles threatens to return home in order to spite Agamemnon; but it would be contrary to his whole nature to choose the negation of glory, and in the end he returns to the battle and to his inevitable death. It is of the essence of Achilles that he has to make this choice between glory and homecoming: it is of the essence of Odysseus that he insists on having both, however long it takes.

In the *Iliad* Achilles makes arrangements for his bones to be buried with those of Patroclus. Looking back in the *Odyssey*, the ghost of Agamemnon in the underworld tells how all this was fulfilled:

> Your white ashes lie   in this golden urn, Achilles,
> indivisibly blended   with the burnt bones of Patroclus.
> Near lies Antilochus,   the comrade you honoured most,
> once Patroclus was lost.   The pick of us Achaean soldiers
> raised a splendid   burial-barrow over you
> on a prominent point   by the broad Hellespont,
> easily visible   from afar to men sailing the ocean,
> both those of these days   and generations not yet born.

The silhouette of the hills to the north and west of Troy are crowned by several artificial mounds which can be seen from the sea or from the city itself. And throughout the surrounding area, known as the Troad, there are dozens of other small mounds or tumuli, called in Turkish *tepe*. Some go back as far as 3000 BC, to the time of the first primitive town at Troy; many date from Hellenistic and Roman times. Later ages have been unable to resist the temptation to identify particular tumuli with the tomb of Hector, the tomb of Ajax, the tomb of Antilochus and so forth.

The tomb of Achilles has always exercised a special fascination. Already by 600 BC, colonisers from nearby Lesbos had founded the town Achilleion near to what they took to be his burial mound. Then in 334 BC, when Alexander the Great crossed the Hellespont, he adorned Achilles' tomb with flowers and perfumes and, according to some sources, danced naked round it. The first recorded visitor of

The mouth of the Dardanelles with the Scamander flowing in, engraved in 1798. In the foreground is the tepe *known as the 'Tomb of Ajax'.*

modern times was a French plant collector, Pierre Belon, in August 1548. (After years spent collecting botanical specimens in Asia and Arabia he was killed by robbers when gathering herbs in the Bois de Boulogne.) Like most early travellers, Belon took the ruins of Alexandria Troas, a large city on the coast well south of Troy, founded after the death of Alexander, to be Troy itself. In 1613 the ebullient English traveller Thomas Coryate enthused:

> It grieved me to my heart that I could not learne either by inscriptions, or by any other meanes, whose Monuments these were: for it is vaine to be induced by conjectures, to say they were these or these mens; onely I hope no man will taxe me of a rash opinion if I beleeve one of them might be the Monument of king Ilus, the Enlarger of the citie of Troy; for I remember that Homer saith in his eleventh Aeneid that Ilus was buried in the open, as this was; and that another of them might be the Monument of king Priamus, it is not altogether unlikely, for Virgil writeth. . .

The burial place of Achilles was, in fact, most often identified with a large tumulus near the tip of Cape Kum Kale at the very opening of the Dardanelles, which archaeologists have now shown to date from the fifth century BC. Its excavation by the Frenchman Lechevallier in 1785 produced a fascinating example of archaeology inspiring a poet's imagination. Within the barrow Lechevallier found two broad stones leaning together over a statuette of Athena, and a metal urn decorated with vine leaves which contained cremated bones. Goethe was reading Lechevallier in 1798 while he was working on his epic

83

Achilleis, a fragmentary continuation of the *Iliad*. As Achilles stands inside the half-finished barrow, Goethe has him give Athena (disguised as Antilochus) instructions for his own burial there:

> At the tomb's mid-point roof over the urn securely –
> And see, I have set two slabs aside, unearthed whilst digging,
> Massive things. . .
>
>   Use these,
> That I set aside, and raise them and stand them together
> For a solid tent. And place the urn beneath
> In secret safekeeping, to the distant end of time.

With characteristic drama, Fuseli here represents a scene from the Iliad – *Achilles cutting a lock from his hair at the funeral pyre of his friend Patroclus.*

Athena goes on to console him for his early death, assuring him that his tomb will serve sailors as a landmark in all ages to come.

Goethe's reading of Homer points up the importance of place to the Romantic sensibility. He never went to the Troad or to Greece, but he felt very close to the *Odyssey* when he was in Sicily, which (in competition with Corfu) has often been equated with the island of the Phaeacians. He was strongly affected when he visited the public gardens of Palermo:

> That magic garden had made too deep an impression on me. The waves along the northern horizon that were so dark as to be almost black, the peculiar smell of the sea in its haze – all this brought back the island of the blessed Phaeacians to my senses and my memory. I hurried at once to buy a copy of Homer, read the book in question with great edification, and translated aloud and impromptu for Kniep. . . . I was persuaded that I could have no better commentary on the *Odyssey* than these living localities themselves.

THE GATES OF THE BLACK SEA

New archaeological finds in 1986 have almost certainly established the original site of the town of Achilleion. Professor Manfred Korfmann of the University of Tübingen spent six years exploring the area around the promontory of Beşik Tepe on the coast to the southwest of Troy. Up on the headland he found fortifications of a kind especially associated with Lesbos and pottery of the early seventh century BC. This means that the settlers from Lesbos, within a century of Homer, took the tomb of Achilles to be either the tumulus on the headland (which as Korfmann has shown in fact goes back to the time of the earliest city at Troy), or another one half a mile inland, called Beşik Sivritepe. Korfmann has made other exciting discoveries, including an earlier cemetery, probably for merchants, on the beach beneath Beşik Tepe. This dates from the period in which the Homeric Trojan War, if there ever was one, should be placed.

It was natural that Korfmann should wish to relate these discoveries to the city at the heart of the whole area. In 1988, working in close collaboration with the Turkish archaeological authorities, he embarked on a twenty-year project to excavate the city that for more than 2000 years dominated the Troad and gave it its name – the great mound of Hisarlık, as it is spelt in the modern Turkish orthography established by Ataturk. (It is pronounced 'Hiss-áre-look'.) This lies at the end of a ridge that stretches out into the alluvial plain deposited over the millennia by the river Scamander before it runs into the sea at the western mouth of the Dardanelles. From the fields of barley, cotton and tomatoes that cover the plain, Hisarlık looks like a promontory overgrown with scrub and small trees. These have established themselves in the century since Heinrich Schliemann's diggings for Troy created hillocks out of his refuse-heaps.

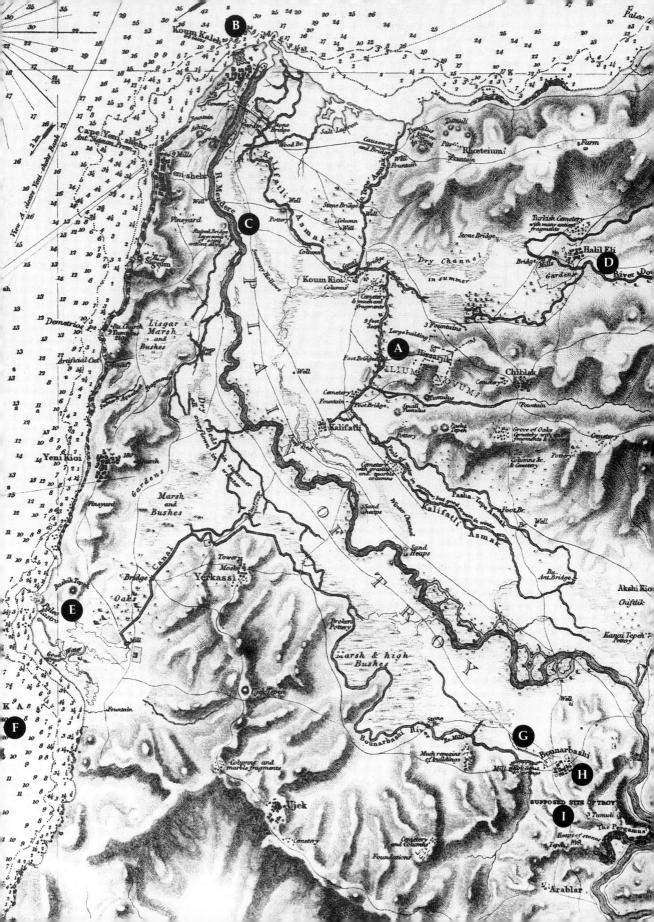

RIGHT] *A rural scene beneath the walls of Troy. The acropolis of Hisarlık rises on the left.*

LEFT] *The map of the Trojan Plain drawn by Midshipman (later Vice-Admiral) Thomas Abel Brimage Spratt in 1839, and still the best. The places referred to in the text are:*

A *Hisarlık – shown by Schliemann to be Troy*

B *Cape Kum Kale – the southern lip of the Dardanelles*

C *River Scamander (Menderes Çay) - the course of the river has since been diverted further east*

D *River Simois (Dümrek Su)*

E *Beşik Tepe*

F *Beşik Bay*

G *The Forty Eyes (Kırk Göz)*

H *The village of Pınarbaşı*

I *Balli Dağ – thought by Spratt to be Troy*

Professor Manfred Korfmann is the first archaeologist to be given permission to excavate Troy for fifty years. He has at his disposal the latest in computerised sounding equipment and in earth-moving machinery; and his team will bring to bear the related sciences of paleobotany, physical anthropology and geophysics. Professor Korfmann has already started to explore outside the walls as well as within the citadel. His project is to study the life and ecology of the whole community. Outside the area of the tourist site there are many acres of cornfields where remains from Roman times, and indeed from the age of Mycene, lie only a couple of feet beneath the surface.

These excavations will be different from all previous explorations at Hisarlık and indeed in this whole area, because they do not take Homer's Troy as their starting point. Professor Korfmann is by training a prehistorian, specialising in the earliest periods of the archaeology of Anatolia (Western Turkey), with a particular interest in migrations, trade and relations between Europe and Asia. For this study, the mouth of the Dardanelles is a key.

Back in Mycenean times the Greeks had already ventured to the area around the Black Sea, attracted by the possibilities of trade: gold from the Caucasus, copper from Northern Anatolia, horses from the Pontic steppes and amber from the Baltic. During Homer's day new colonies were founded all round the shores of the Black Sea. Modern cities in Turkey, Bulgaria and the Soviet Union derive their names from those early Greek colonies – Sinop (Sinope), Trabzon (Trapezos), Feodosiya (Theodosia), Nesebur (Mesembria).

87

The only access from the Mediterranean to the Black Sea is through two straits, the Dardanelles and the Bosphorus. Between them lies the Sea of Marmara. Troy is at the western mouth of the Dardanelles, where it enters the Aegean. At the further end of the Sea of Marmara, on the Bosphorus, the Greeks planted the city of Byzantium, destined to become Constantinople and then Istanbul.

The Dardanelles are tricky to navigate: many major rivers, including the Danube, flow into the Black Sea and out through the strait into the Mediterranean, creating a current which flows at 5 kph. When combined with the *Meltemi*, the winds which blow constantly from the northwest at certain times of the year, the straits used to become impassable. Sailing ships, especially in the days before keels were invented, were often held up for weeks at a time in the bay to the south of the entrance. Professor Korfmann claims that Troy's wealth and importance came about through providing pilots and supplies to ships held up in this way. He has excavated on the coast west of Hisarlık to see if Beşik Bay (now silted up) was once the harbour of Troy, where shipping had to wait. The city itself was built several miles inland so that it would not be open to surprise attack.

THE TROJAN WARS

As Hector's proposal of a burial mound in the *Iliad* illustrates, the *tepes* all round the shores of the Troad are a sort of boast to those who sail by. They mark an area where many have died over the last 4000 years and more. Professor Korfmann reckons that there has probably been at least one Trojan war in most centuries, if those fought over the Bosphorus are included. In this century 300,000 died in the Gallipoli campaign in 1915. Before that, the Ottoman Turks conquered Constantinople in 1453, after taking the Troad first. In 1203 the Fourth Crusade sacked Constantinople instead of going to Jerusalem. Back in the seventh century BC, soon after Homer, settlers from Athens and from Lesbos fought for control of the Troad. And so on, back into prehistory.

Schliemann and his successor Dörpfeld thought that they had found nine Troys, from Troy I of about 3000 BC down to Troy IX, built by the Romans in the first centuries after Christ. It is now reckoned, however, that over 40 rebuildings of the city can be distinguished. As each one added to the layers below it, the mound eventually reached a height of about 20 metres above the original level, as high as a four-storey building. Wealthy but vulnerable, successive generations of Trojans fortified and refortified their city. This has made it one of the greatest – and most complex – archaeological sites in the world. Korfmann compares digging here to cutting into a cake: in the stratification of Schliemann's great trench he can see the history of the many Troys.

Across time many nations have lived here, many have fought and died here. Some have built the place up, others have destroyed it. Ironically, Troy has even been destroyed by those who came to honour her. Schliemann, in the course of his epoch-making

An old Turkish cemetery near the mouth of the Dardanelles, testament to the many Trojan wars.

discoveries, demolished much of the upper levels of the ancient city and left the place a bewildering maze of dips and heaps – 'the ruins of a ruin' as it has been called. Nearly 2000 years earlier, the Julio-Claudian emperors of Rome decided to lay out a great new city here in honour of their ancestors: they traced their line back to Aeneas, the cousin of Hector, who, according to legend, fled from the destruction of Troy to found a new dynasty in Italy. 'The Romans put a lot of money into this place,' as Professor Korfmann put it. In order to build a great temple to Athena – or Minerva as they called her – they levelled off much of the Greek city which then stood on top of the 40 earlier Troys. Like Schliemann, they destroyed much that would be of the greatest interest to a modern archaeologist.

Korfmann's most recent excavations outside the citadel have uncovered the foundation walls of Roman houses neatly cut down into remains of Troy VI and VII, the cities that date from the Mycenean Age. This was the Troy of Aeneas – the Troy which became the subject of Homer's epic, the Troy destroyed by Odysseus.

CLEARING THE BASTION
The romantic quest to find this 'real Troy', as well as the landmarks of Homer's Trojan War, obsessed both the ancient Greek world and the

explorers and antiquarians of the last 500 years. Byron was held up for seventeen days at the mouth of the Dardanelles in April 1810. He was, however, bored and called the plain of Troy 'a fine field for conjecture and snipe-shooting'. Yet later in *Don Juan* he wrote:

> . . . I stood upon Achilles' tomb
> And heard Troy doubted: Time will doubt of Rome.

And near the end of his life he wrote in his diary:

> We *do* care about 'the authenticity of the tale of Troy'. I have stood upon that plain daily for more than a month, in 1810, and if anything diminished my pleasure, it was that the blaggard Bryant had impugned its veracity . . . I still venerated the grand original as *the truth of history* (in material *facts* and of *place*).

The eighteenth-century antiquarian Jacob Bryant had written a book (1796) with the pithy title 'A Dissertation concerning the War of Troy, and the Expedition of the Grecians, as described by Homer, showing that no such Expedition was Ever Undertaken, and that no such City of Phrygia Existed.'

Do we, then, have to take sides, and either agree with Byron that Homer's Trojan War was 'the truth of history', or with Bryant that 'no such City Existed'? As recently as 1985 the side of history was vigorously and attractively championed by Michael Wood. In his enormously popular television series (and accompanying book) *In Search of the Trojan War* he has told once again the story of how Heinrich Schliemann, with Homer in one hand, was determined to prove the truth of the *Iliad*, and how he struck gold in the mound of Hisarlık. The rest is archaeology. Schliemann made Troy sufficiently celebrated to be cited as the last word of Heywood Floyd's message to David Bowman on board *Discovery*:

> We do not know if, out on the moons of Saturn, you will meet with good or with evil – or only with ruins a thousand times older than Troy.

Mistakenly believing that Priam's Troy would be the very lowest levels of the accumulated cities of Hisarlık, Schliemann destroyed large parts of Troy VI and VII, the Troys of the Mycenean era, and hastily discarded as rubbish virtually all traces of Troy VIII, the city of 'New Ilium'. This was founded by Greeks in about 750 BC, using the huge ruined walls of the earlier Troy, which had been deserted for some 350 years. Yet if Homer ever visited Troy, then this is the city he would have seen. If Homer lived on Chios it would be odd if he had *not* visited Troy – Chios lies not far to the south, with only the island of Lesbos in between. In Aeschylus' play *Agamemnon* it takes at least ten beacons to flash the news of the sack of Troy to Argos in the Peloponnese. A beacon chain to Homer on Chios would only have to go: Troy → Mount Ida (Kaz Dağ) → Lesbos → Chios.

Professor Korfmann presumes that a major Greek expedition besieged and sacked Troy in the late Mycenean period. If asked 'Was

A defiant bastion of Troy VI seen from below. First exposed by Schliemann, it was cleared afresh by Professor Korfmann's team in 1988.

there a Trojan war?' he replies, 'There were many Trojan wars'; for him Homer's war is only one of them. His close acquaintance with the area has, however, persuaded him – as it did Professor John Cook, author of the authoritative book *The Troad* – that Homer, the poet of the *Iliad*, had visited this place, and that he set his poem within this very landscape. The relationship between the *Iliad* and the real world according to them is quite different from the relationship so passionately advocated by Schliemann, and more recently by Michael Wood. What is real is not the history of 500 years earlier, but the landscape of Homer's own day, feeding his creative mind.

The city which Homer would have seen in about 700 BC was built amongst the monumental remains of more ancient Troys, especially Troy VI. Professor Korfmann's team has newly cleared and cleaned one of the bastions of this period, originally uncovered by Schliemann. Seen from below, it is possible to grasp a fragmentary idea of how Troy's fortifications would have looked to an attacker in the plain – an Odysseus' eye view. Korfmann hopes eventually to clear away Schliemann's mounds, and so reveal the whole view of this stretch of the walls. If he achieves this, Troy, as yet relatively unknown, will come to rival Mycene as a tourist attraction.

The Greeks of Homer's day built their new houses against bastions such as this one. These earlier monuments would have been impressive even in their ruined state – the remains of massive walls

91

The first city of Smyrna surrounded by the suburbs of modern Izmir. In the eighth century BC the dip between these two hills was a harbour (the coast is now about half a mile away).

constructed before the age of iron, nevertheless still standing without the aid of the clamps that were a recent innovation. These more ancient constructions evoke Homer's epithets such as 'Troy of the fine masonry', 'Troy of the broad streets' and 'Troy of the tall towers'.

In Homer's creative imagination the Troy of the distant past has become a fine civilised place, a good place to live in, if only it were at peace. His imagination must surely have also been fed by the fine cities of his own world, such as Smyrna, about 300 kilometres south by road, and his birthplace according to ancient tradition. Homer's Smyrna was besieged and destroyed by Lydian enemies in about 600 BC; so the *Iliad* in a sense foreshadows its fate. About 300 years later, a new Smyrna was founded a few kilometres away, and with time that has become the modern Izmir.

Izmir is Turkey's third largest city, with a population of two million; and, as the headquarters for the southeast sector of NATO, it buzzes with foreign military personnel. Twentieth-century suburbs have spread out to surround the first Smyrna. What was originally a headland is now an olive-covered island among a sea of houses. Excavations in the 1960s exposed impressive walls, regular streets and handsome buildings. This is how it was in Homer's day, in peacetime, before the Lydians arrived.

Homer uses fitting epithets not only for the city of Troy, but for the whole area – 'with rich soil', 'good for grazing horses', 'wind-swept'. In his poem *Ulysses*, Tennyson has Odysseus recall:

[I] drunk delight of battle with my peers,
Far on the ringing plains of windy Troy.

You have only to stand on the walls, or to notice the bent shape of the trees, to realise how appropriate this description is.

THE PINARBAŞI TECHNIQUE

We found the conclusion reached by others such as Cook and Korfmann, who know the Troad well, irresistible: Homer had himself been here and envisaged his *Iliad* within this landscape. The realities of topography enhance the details of the poem. For example, the *Iliad* makes more sense if the shore where Homer envisaged the Achaean ships is taken to be Beşik Bay. This means that he placed the fighting in his poetic eye (whether or not it actually happened) to the west of Troy, not, as has been usually supposed, to the north.

One landmark above all in the *Iliad* in our view confirms the belief that Homer visited the Troad for himself. About eight kilometres south of the city is a hill called Ballı Dağ, and at its foot, near the modern village of Pınarbaşı (pronounced Pernárbasher), is a half-mile string of remarkable springs known as the Kırk Göz – 'Forty Eyes'. Along their accumulating stream the land is lusciously green and fertile. The villagers tend their garden plots, horses graze, tall

'Back in peace, before. . .' The pool by the lowest and most copious of the 'Forty Eyes' of Pınarbaşı.

A favourite washing place at another smaller 'Eye'.

poplars rustle in the breeze, and the birds make a continuous song. There are many small watering-holes ('forty' in Turkish simply means 'a lot') and about a dozen larger ones, where the water gurgles to the surface. Several of these are bustling centres of activity: shepherds bring their sheep and goats to drink, farmers drive their tractors into the shallow water to replenish their great irrigation drums, and children congregate to fill jugs and jars, to wash and splash happily. For, unlike most springs, these run with warm water. This is why the women from all the local villages come here to do their washing. Squatting by the running water, they soap the clothes and bash the dirt out of them with wooden bats, before rinsing them. As they work, they chatter and laugh in this scene of tranquillity.

The villagers of Pınarbaşı are proud of their Forty Eyes, and especially of the way the warm waters steam in winter. It is hard not to recall Homer's springs of Scamander, one hot with steam, the other cold like ice, the washing-places of the Trojan women. As John Cook writes:

> Of all the curiosities of the Troad the Kırk Göz is perhaps the most celebrated, and if we are disposed to look for a natural feature that could have inspired the poetic description, only inveterate prejudice can deny that honour to these springs.

Lechavallier recognised this inspiration back in 1795 and took the remains of a citadel on Ballı Dağ to be Troy. It remained the favourite candidate until Schliemann came along. As he triumphantly pointed

94

out, the terrain of Ballı Dağ would make it impossible for Hector and Achilles to run round it, while the circuit of Hisarlık would be quite feasible. On the other hand, there are no interesting springs outside Hisarlık, though Schliemann desperately argued the case for an old, blocked-up trickle that he found. Both Lechavallier and Schliemann would not be content unless the poem was geographically and hydrologically accurate.

Yet neither the Kırk Göz nor Schliemann's trickle can supply both hot and cold springs. Professor Cook measured the Pınarbaşı springs several times in different seasons in the 1960s with an untested baker's thermometer from Boots: he found that there was no variety of temperatures among them, and that they always registered 62° Fahrenheit. Almost 40 kilometres away up in the mountains, however, far from any village washing-places, the springs of the Scamander/Menderes do indeed vary in temperature.

The *Iliad* is poetry and is the product of a creative, transforming mind. Homer saw the real walls of Hisarlık, built into the recently refounded Troy VIII; he saw the real Kırk Göz, 8 kilometres away; and he may have seen or heard about the springs in the mountains. Each insinuated its way into his all-absorbing mind and were put together – with a cold spring to balance the hot – to form the setting for the death of Hector, a setting which helps to create one of the great moments in the literature of the world. Real places go in, but something even more real, something adaptable across times and places far beyond, emerges.

The insight that real places fed Homer's poetic genius was perceived as early as the eighteenth century by Robert Wood who visited the area in 1750, and whose *Essay on the original genius of Homer* (published in 1775 after his death) had a profound influence on the Romantic movement. On his travels in Asia Minor, Wood found solid evidence that the *Iliad* and the *Odyssey* were set not in a fantastical world, but were based on details of a real time and place. (Contrast the world of *The Lord of the Rings* or of *The Chronicles of Narnia*, for instance.) 'The *Iliad*,' he wrote, 'has new beauties on the banks of Scamander, and the *Odyssey* is most pleasing in the countries where Ulysses travelled and Homer sang.'

The Forty Eyes of Pınarbaşı give a new beauty to the washing-places that the women of Troy used in the days of peace. Today their peace once more is fragile and may be threatened at any time by industrial development, just as the nearby coast has been wrecked by a monstrous cement-works – providing perhaps an analogy with the way that the Achaeans came to destroy the peace of Troy. First among them, Odysseus earned the epithet the 'sacker of cities'.

ODYSSEUS BEARING GIFTS

Later on in the day that Demodocus sings of the quarrel between Odysseus and Achilles, Odysseus, who is still anonymous, has gained enough stature with the Phaeacians to make a request:

At the village of Pınarbaşı is a plant for bottling the water and for packing agricultural produce.

A scene from the spaghetti epic La guerra di Troia *made in 1961. Steve Reeves starred as Aeneas.*

'Now shift to the story   of how the wooden horse
was first worked by   Epeius, helped by Athena,
then how it made its way   through the deceit of Odysseus
inside the city, packed   with the troops who sacked Troy.
If you can tell that tale   as it deserves, I'd assert
to the world that you are   a poet inspired by the god.'
So he spoke. The poet,   summoning the Muse, started the story
at the point when   the Achaean army embarked
and sailed away in their ships,   leaving their camp in flames.
Meanwhile the men who   stayed with famous Odysseus
huddled inside the horse   in the heart of the town of Troy.
They themselves had dragged   the horse inside their citadel.
So there it stood,   and the Trojans gathered round
divided in debate   between three ways of treating it:
either to thrust a spear   through the wooden womb,
or to bring it to the brink   and hurl it off a cliff,
or else to let it rest,   to placate the powers above.
And in the end this plan   was destined to win the day,
for it was fated   that the city would be sacked, once

it had harboured the horse   of wood, where lurked within
the chief Achaeans,   dealers of death and destruction.
Next he told of how   the Achaeans sacked the city,
pouring out of the horse   from their cavernous ambush;
how here and everywhere   they ransacked steep Troy.
He told how Odysseus   the warrior went with Menelaus
To the palace of prince   Deiphobus, and endured
through the fiercest   fighting he ever met with.
Yet with the help of Athena   he survived victorious.

The most famous of all the stories of the Trojan War is surely that of
the wooden horse. James Joyce saw it as a prototype of the tank:
'They are both shells containing armed warriors.' The horse is insep-
arable from the havoc which issued from it – 'The broken wall, the
burning roof and tower' in W. B. Yeats's phrase. In recent years it
has provided the copy for cartoons and advertisements; while at the
other extreme of sensibility, the horror unleashed from the horse
infuses the East German Christa Wolf's novel *Cassandra*, published
in 1983. In another trouble-spot of the world, policemen, hidden in a
covered vehicle, emerged and opened fire without warning in the
Athlone suburb of Cape Town on 15 October 1985. This shocking
contemporary re-enactment became known as the Trojan Horse
incident.

A contemporary Trojan Horse.

BRU/CPT01 : AM-SOUTH AFRICA; CAPETOWN, SOUTH AFRICA, OCT. 16 - Police in
Capetown use Trojan Horse tactics to counter rioters, riding through the
streets hidden in a truck and emerging with shotguns when stoned by
demonstrators **yesterday**.
REUTER   fr/amk/Rubython/SA OUT   1985.

The wooden horse was Odysseus' greatest act of craft and cunning at Troy: it was for this deceit that Dante placed him in his *Inferno*. Odysseus asks Demodocus to recount this particular story because the struggle inside the walls was 'the fiercest fighting he ever met with'. Yet he was not famed, at least in the *Odyssey*, for particular feats during Troy's fall, but rather for being the leading member of the pack, always there in the thick of it, the 'sacker of cities'. For example, it was Menelaus who mutilated Deiphobus, the prince who had married Helen after the death of Paris: Odysseus – at least according to the usual story – merely incited him to the deed and looked on in approval. In one version of the story, however, it was Odysseus, rather than Neoptolemus, who threw Astyanax, the young son of Hector, off the battlements of Troy.

The sack of Troy has more often been seen from the perspective of the victims than of the victors, especially by those nations, above all the Romans, who have traced their ancestry back to the Trojans. These and subsequent events place Odysseus in a less favourable light than in the *Odyssey*. In Euripides' powerful (and somewhat neglected) tragedy *Hecuba*, first performed in Athens in 423 BC, it is Odysseus, 'that hypocrite with honeyed tongue', who persuades the mob of Greek soldiers that the Trojan queen Hecuba's daughter Polyxena should be sacrificed at the tomb of Achilles. With relish

This tall clay jar with scenes modelled in relief, found on the island of Mykonos, was made in about 675 BC, close to the time of Homer. The Trojan Horse on the neck, and the gruesome scenes below of the sack of the city, are in spirit strikingly like those described in the Iliad.

Odysseus takes upon himself the task of fetching the virgin to the slaughter.

The best-known and most influential account of the wooden horse and of the sack of Troy comes in the second book of Virgil's *Aeneid*. Virgil, Rome's great disciple of Homer, had not completed his epic poem, which tells of the wanderings of Aeneas, a prince of Troy, when he died in 19 BC. Like Odysseus, Aeneas faces many adventures. He is not destined, however, to return to his former home, but to found a nation, Rome. When Aeneas reaches Carthage on the North African coast he tells his own story to Dido, the queen, just as Odysseus does to king Alcinous in the *Odyssey*. He starts with the false departure of the Greeks. As in Demodocus' version, there is a debate about what to do with the monstrous horse which the Greeks have left behind. The priest Laocoon warns:

> Trojans, wretched fools, have you gone crazy?
> You believe they've really gone? You think there's any present
> from the Greeks without a trick? Is this the old Ulysses
> that you know? . . .
> Some deceit is lurking there. Don't trust the horse, I tell you.
> I'm afraid of Greeks, yes, even when they're offering gifts.

Timeo Danaos et dona ferentes: as famous a tag as any in Latin. The Trojans are swayed against Laocoon by the false stories of Sinon, a Greek who pretends to have been captured against his will. One of Sinon's main tactics to gain credence is to abuse Odysseus; he even pretends to be related to Palamedes, Odysseus' greatest rival whose death he had brought about by trickery. Characteristically, Odysseus is prepared for anyone to say anything they like against him, provided he gets his own way in the end. Contrast Achilles: as Virgil's contemporary poet Horace pointed out, Achilles 'would not have hidden in the horse, . . . nor attempted to deceive the Trojans as they enjoyed their ill-timed celebrations.'

It was Virgil, rather than any Greek source, who planted the image of Troy in flames in the world's imagination, and literature rather than history that made this one out of Troy's many sackings so important. Against the backcloth of the burning city Virgil sets Aeneas, carrying his old father Anchises and his household gods, as he departs to found a new Troy that will become Rome. A dream-figure of the dead Hector has handed him the sacred flame of the hearth of Troy, which will eventually burn in the temple of the Vestal Virgins. The story of the small band of survivors escaping the city's sack has inspired works of art from the paintings of Raphael and Elsheimer to the operas of Hector Berlioz and Michael Tippett.

It was given a new twist in 1935 by the French writer Jean Giraudoux in his play *Le guerre de Trois n'aura pas lieu* (translated into English by Christopher Fry as *Tiger at the Gates*). Giraudoux was building on an episode in the *Iliad* that displayed Odysseus' reputation as an ambassador. In Homer's version, the Trojan elder, Antenor, describes a failed attempt at negotiations:

When subtle Odysseus   stood up to make a speech,
he inclined his head   down towards the ground,
and held the speaker's sceptre   without waving it to and fro,
but all stiffly   like some nervous novice.
You might have taken him   for a sullen senseless lout; but
when once he unleashed   the massive voice from his chest
and his words swirled   like the flakes of falling snow,
then nobody could hold   a candle to Odysseus,
and so then we soon   forgot our first impressions.

Giraudoux himself was a diplomat as well as a playwright. Disillusioned with the efforts of the League of Nations to preserve peace, he made up an encounter which dramatised the empty diplomatic posturing that failed to prevent war. His Ulysses is not unkind, but he is a hard-bitten cynic:

> You are a young man Hector! . . . On the eve of every war it is customary for the two leaders of the hostile parties to meet, alone in some innocent village, on a terrace by a lake, in the corner of a garden. And they agree that war is the worst blight in the world. . . . And, warmed by the sun, relaxed by a fine wine, they do not see in the face before them a single feature which justifies hatred. . . . And they are truly full of peace, of desire for peace. . . . And they shake hands and part, feeling like brothers. . . . And the following day the war begins.

Hector and Ulysses from a 1963 Paris production of Jean Giraudoux's La Guerre de Troie n'aura pas lieu.

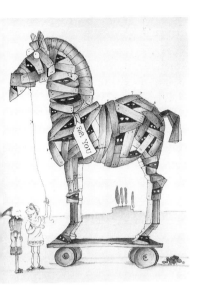

'Never trust a Greek. . .!'

THE TROJAN WOMEN

Scholars are not unaffected by their times, though they all too rarely make their contemporary preoccupations explicit. W. B. Stanford in *The Ulysses Theme*, writing when the events of the Second World War were still fresh, is candid when he considers the Odysseus of Euripides' play *Trojan Women*. He speaks of Euripides' Odysseus as:

> the extreme type of the chauvinistic and militaristic power-politician, correct as any Nazi Gauleiter and as impervious to personal or emotional appeals . . . Most sinister of all in the light of recent events in Europe is his convenient doctrine that to class people as 'barbarians' is a valid reason for treating them as beasts.

In 415 BC, the year of the first production of *Trojan Women*, Euripides had fresh in his mind the ruthless massacre of the people of the island of Melos, a cold-blooded demonstration of Athenian imperial power, which had taken place the previous year. Giraudoux and Stanford both translated it into terms of their own day. Since 1945, however, the diplomats and even the Gauleiters have been overshadowed by the threat of extinction. A thermo-nuclear wooden horse would leave no Odysseus to be further transformed. Troy in flames has inevitably become a premonition of the whole world in flames. It is only appropriate that a recent Japanese production of *Trojan Women* was set before the charred remains of Hiroshima.

The theatre-poet Tony Harrison brings this out in his own version of *Trojan Women* (yet to be staged), which is set outside a nuclear missile base. Odysseus does not actually come on stage in this play, but lurks malevolently in the background, the political schemer behind the scenes. Queen Hecuba hears that she has been allotted to Odysseus as his prisoner:

> *Hecuba*   And who gets me with one foot in the grave?
> *Talthybius* You go to Odysseus. You're Odysseus' slave.
> *Hecuba*   A slave to that dirty despicable liar. That
>   despiser of justice, that defiler of right.
>   His tongue made white black, black white.
>   Sisters sisters weep for me. Of you all
>   I'm brought the lowest with furthest to fall.

Andromache, the widow of Hector, is brought on stage on a cart with her baby son Astyanax – she is a piece of baggage for the victors. Then the herald Talthybius arrives to tell her that the Greeks have decided to kill Astyanax. Only one line is needed to say who it was who advocated this repulsive act:

> *Talthybius* They're going to kill him since you force me to
>   speak.
> *Andromache* That's worse than me being raped by that
>   Greek.
> *Talthybius* There was a debate and Odysseus won.
> *Andromache* What worse can happen now? My son! My son!

The Odysseus of the *Odyssey* is cunning and relentless towards his enemies, yet he is not the villain that Euripides paints him, the *éminence noire* who manipulates others into pressing the button. When Demodocus recites for him the story of the wooden horse and of his exploits, he does not sit there proudly preening himself: he weeps. At this point Homer produces one of his most breathtaking similes. Rather as many of the similes of the *Iliad* are drawn from the peacetime rural world, the world of the *Odyssey* and of Pınarbaşı, so this one evokes the wartime world of the *Iliad*:

So the poet told the story.   Odysseus dissolved:
the tears trickled   down and drenched his cheeks.
As a wife might weep   clasping her beloved husband,
when he has fallen   before his walls and his people,
keeping back the cruel day   from his land and its children;
she sees him in his death throes   and, wrapping herself around
him, shrieks shrill lament;   but her captors come up
and beat her on the back   with their spears, and the shoulders;
they seize her as a slave   for a life full of pain and labour;
her cheeks are wasted away   furrowed with pitiful grief:
so Odysseus shed   tear drops, water of pity.

A fourteenth-century Italian manuscript showing Odysseus and his men leaving Troy for the fateful journey home.

This is like Andromache; at the same time it is every woman whose life is ruined by war. Homer's Odysseus is big-hearted enough to sympathise with the dark side of his hour of triumph.

102

5 DOUBLING MALEIA

So many complex monsters that prevent us from remembering that he too was a man struggling in the world with a soul and body.

George Seferis

King Alcinous is the only one who sees Odysseus weeping, and he decides that it is now time for the stranger to identify himself:

> The moment has come,   so tell your story truly.
> What countries were you   driven to while wandering?
> Tell of the towns   and about their inhabitants,
> and whether they were wild,   violent and lawless,
> or hospitable hosts   fair and god-fearing.
> And say why you sorrow   and weep deep inside, when you
> hear tell of the fate   that the Argives gave Troy.

So two days after his arrival, now that he has established himself as a man who can live up to his name, Odysseus declares himself:

> I am called Odysseus, son   of Laertes, so celebrated
> for tricks and deceit   that my glory reaches the skies.
> I live on Ithaca. . . .

His bard-like narrative of his wanderings then takes up the last third of the first half of the poem. If we imagine a performance beginning at six o'clock in the evening, then Odysseus' wanderings might well have lasted from about one o'clock till half past four in the morning.

Odysseus and his companions in their twelve ships (fifty men in each) start out from Troy, (the very first word is *Iliothen*, 'from Ilion'); and their first port of call is Ismarus where they sack the city of the Cicones, but incur heavy losses. This was a real place in Thrace, allied to Troy. They are then driven across the Aegean by a storm:

> Now I might have made it   unharmed to my homeland,
> had not hurricane and current   stopped me doubling Maleia,
> as I came round the cape,   and thrust me off course past Cythera.

Before the building of the Corinth canal, the turning-point of any journey from the east to the west of the Greek mainland was the rounding of Cape Maleia, the southeast tip of the Peloponnese. There is a Greek proverb which goes back to ancient times which says 'When you round Cape Maleia forget the folks at home', for it was and still is a notorious hazard for shipping.

LEFT] *The dangerous east side of Cape Maleia, with the lighthouse.*

BELOW LEFT] *The west side with the shrine of thanksgiving.*

THE VERGE OF IMAGINATION

Today, only two buildings cling to the massive jagged rocks of Cape Maleia. On the eastern side is a lighthouse to warn sailors, and high up on the west a tiny white Byzantine chapel stands as a token of thanksgiving. Once upon a time, we were told, three monks tended the chapel. Only a short while ago there certainly was a lighthouse keeper who must have made his way along the narrow and perilous goat-path from Velanidhia, the last village before the cape. Now the lighthouse is solar-powered, but little else is changed.

It is a 40-minute drive along a dirt-track from Neapolis, the nearest town to Velanidhia. There is nowhere to stay and no shop when you get there: only white houses perched precipitously on the hillside above a sheltered harbour. We chugged out of here at six in the morning in a fishing boat with the captain, Iannis, and Panayiotis. Georgios also came for the ride. Warmed by tiny cups of sweet Greek coffee, we sat and watched for more than two hours as the two fishermen pulled in an apparently endless yellow net from a bottomless blue sea. There was no wind. With the net and its catch safely heaped on board, we restarted the engine and approached the cape. Quite suddenly there were white-capped waves and the boat began to rock nauseously from side to side. However calm the day, Iannis told us, the sea is always rough doubling Maleia.

There is a good meteorological explanation for this phenomenon, yet even today the cape retains its mystery. One-armed Georgios told us that the three monks had once been pirate-captains. A terrible storm off Maleia smashed their three frigates and they were the only survivors; they became monks and, according to our storyteller, as

RIGHT] *Iannis the fisherman off Cape Maleia.*

long as they lived, not a single boat went down off the cape. Iannis declared the tale a mere myth, but the others insisted that it was history.

For all three of them, Odysseus was no more than a vaguely recalled name from their schooldays; but they all agreed that he had only to round the cape, and the rest of his voyage to Ithaca would have been plain sailing. Instead, he was carried south, past the island of Cythera, and off the map of the human world. Maleia marks the division between reality and imagination. It would be nine years before Odysseus returned to anywhere that can be found in an atlas.

The poem continues:

> Nine days I was dragged   along by galling gales
> over the fish-filled ocean,   till on the tenth day we sailed
> into Lotus-land,   where fragrant fruit is all they eat.

From now on it is a matter of man-eating giants, of Aeolus who puts the winds in a bag, of Circe who turns humans into swine, of the Sirens who lure men to death with their song, Scylla and Charybdis, and the rest. He even goes to the Underworld, the last place that anyone alive would wish to visit and usually a one-way trip. In the end, Odysseus loses all his men and is washed up on the island of Calypso, where Homer first finds him. These adventures have always been the best-loved part of the *Odyssey*. Many children still first hear of them at primary school, and we hope that they will continue to do so.

In the land of the Lotus-eaters, Odysseus' incautious men try out the fruit and he has to bring them back to the ship by force. Tennyson built a wonderful poem, almost Pre-Raphaelite in its bright languid images, out of this brief incident. It starts with typical Odyssean vigour:

RIGHT] *This burlesque version of Odysseus being offered the magic potion by Circe (with her loom behind her) was painted in Boeotia in about 400 BC.*

ABOVE] *One of Odysseus' men turned into an animal by Circe on another Boeotian cup.*

'Courage' he said, and pointed towards the land,
'This mounting wave will roll us shoreward soon.'

But it soon seems that no one can resist the sensuous narcotic lure of the island:

There is sweet music here that softer falls
Than petals from blown roses on the grass,
Or night-dews on still waters between walls
Of shadowy granite, in a gleaming pass;
Music that gentlier on the spirit lies,
Than tired eyelids upon tir'd eyes. . . .

The poem ends:

Surely surely slumber is more sweet than toil, the shore
Than labour in the deep mid-ocean, wind and wave and oar;
Oh rest ye, brother mariners, we will not wander more.

CYCLOPEAN HOSPITALITY

Unlike Tennyson's, Homer's Odysseus passes on and comes next to the most celebrated of all his adventures, in the cave of the giant one-eyed Cyclops, Polyphemus. Here his endurance is tried to the utmost. Later, at home on Ithaca, he looks back on this as his most testing experience, when he says to himself:

Endure, old heart,   you put up with worse than this
on the day that the   cruel Cyclops crunched
my brave comrades;   yet you endured then,
and your cunning contrived   an escape from the cave of death.

In this episode Odysseus shows his outstanding qualities, not only of endurance but also of craft and cunning. Homer gives Odysseus the epithet that only he merits, *polumetis* 'the man of much *metis*', or cunning.

'To explore strange new worlds; to seek out new life and new civilisations; to boldly go where no man has gone before': Odysseus is often driven against his will, but there is a strong element of the *Starship Enterprise* about his curiosity and his urge, almost that of an anthropologist, to find out about strange people and places. He and his companions land first at an offshore island; but see smoke and hear voices on the mainland. The Captain Kirk mentality then takes over:

The rest of you stay here,   my constant comrades,
I'll go only with   my own ship and its company
to try and test   these unfamiliar men,
to see whether they're wild,   violent and lawless,
or hospitable hosts   fair and god-fearing.

He sees a cave near the shore and sets out with twelve of his men, taking with him provisions and an especially good vintage of wine.

> My bold heart had,   you see, a shrewd suspicion
> that we should meet with a man   clothed with fantastic strength,
> wild and without regard   for civilisation or law.

This is the cave of Polyphemus, of course, a Cyclops who is violent and antisocial even by Cyclopean standards. Instead of making a quick get-away as his companions suggest, Odysseus is curious:

> But no, I wouldn't listen   – though that would have been far
> better –
> I insisted on seeing   and hoping he'd give me guest-gifts.
> But he turned out to be   a far from delightful sight
> for my friends . . .

While he and his men are in the cave, Polyphemus returns with his sheep and goats; he blocks the door with a huge stone, milks his flocks, and only when he lights a fire does he spot his visitors. He begins to question them and Odysseus tells him *some* of the truth. When asked where he has left his ship, however, he tells the straightforward lie that they have been shipwrecked:

> So he spoke, testing me out,   but I was more than his match:
> the reply that I returned   was weighted with tricky words.

Then, all of a sudden, the Cyclops smashes the heads of two of Odysseus' men on the ground, tears them up and eats them raw. After swilling them down with fresh milk he falls asleep. Odysseus has patience:

> In my intrepid spirit   I wanted to get in close,
> unsheathing my sharp sword   and stab him through the breast.
> But a restraining spirit   held me. We would all surely
> die in there, like the others,   since we hadn't the strength
> to shove the vast stone   he used to block the cave-mouth.

Polyphemus sets off in the morning with a merry whistle, and blocks the door for the day. Before he comes back, Odysseus has worked out his plan: to make Polyphemus drunk on the wine as a treat after his meal of man-flesh, and then to blind his single eye using a great stake of olive wood that is lying in the cave. All goes according to plan, Odysseus adding the master stroke to his strategy:

> Three times I topped him up: three times he stupidly swigged it.
> When the vintage had twined   around the Cyclops' mind,
> I began to beguile him   with these winsome words:
> 'You ask for my famous name,   Cyclops, so I shall declare it;
> but to be true to your word,   you must give me a guest-gift.
> Noman is my name.   From birth my father and mother
> and everyone near and dear   have known me as Noman.'
> I spoke. Quick he replied   in a spirit without pity:
> 'Noman shall be munched   last, after all his friends;
> first I'll feast on the rest: that's to be my guest-gift.'

ABOVE] *This powerful picture by Tibaldi of the blinding of Polyphemus was painted in the mid-sixteenth century. Note the leftovers of Odysseus' companions.*

RIGHT] *One of the very earliest illustrations of the story of Odysseus, this was painted in the first half of the seventh century* BC, *and was found at Eleusis near Athens.*

So speaking he slumped   on his back, with his thick neck
turned to one side, as   all-subduing sleep clapped him
in chains. Then the wine   gurgled from his gullet
with lumps of human flesh.   Thus he spewed in his stupor.
Then I thrust that stake   deep under the red embers
to get it glowing . . .

Polyphemus' cries of agony ring out in the night and his neighbouring Cyclopes come running:

'What on earth has stirred you,   Polyphemus, to make this
rumpus
through the deserted night,   spoiling our peaceful sleep?
Surely no one human   is stealing your flocks by force?
Surely no one's slaughtering you   by trickery or battery?'
'My friends,' fierce Polyphemus   called back from in the cave,
'Noman's surely slaughtering me   by trickery not battery.'
They replied with words   which winged their way inside:
'Then if no man's   beating you all by yourself,
there's no easy cure   for a sickness sent by Zeus.
Perhaps lord Poseidon your   father will answer your prayers.'
So saying they went away;   and my heart laughed in glee
to think how my own cunning   and my no man name had foxed
him.

Homer works in an extra twist: the Greek for Noman is *ou tis* (*Outis*). In certain grammatical contexts *ou tis* changes to *me tis* which is the same as *metis*, meaning 'cunning and craft' – Odysseus' special quality. This grammatical change occurs in fact in the reply of the other Cyclopes: 'if no one [*me tis*] is beating you'. Odysseus laughs to himself 'to think how my own cunning [*metis*] and my no man name had foxed him'.

Polyphemus then opens the doorway and hopes to catch the men as they escape:

All this time I was scheming   how best to escape death's door,
and to work a way out   for me and my comrades.
I wove a brain-web   spinning my tricks and cunning –
it was our lives at stake   and a terrible end loomed.

A delightful bronze 'plaque' of one of Odysseus' men escaping from Polyphemus, made in the sixth century BC and found at Delphi. It is only about 10 centimetres long.

'Cunning' here is *metis* once again. Odysseus arranges their escape by strapping them underneath Polyphemus' sheep; when they go out in the morning, Polyphemus feels the backs of his animals only. Odysseus holds on under the ram of the flock, which the giant addresses. The balance of sympathy is shifted:

> I wish that you shared thoughts   and had language like mine,
> so you could show me   where he's lurking from my clutches.

Once Odysseus is safely on board ship, and a little out from the shore he calls out tauntingly:

> So, Cyclops, it wasn't   a weakling's friends you wanted
> to crunch so cruelly   inside your deep cavern, no,
> your wrongs were due   to snare you – and with a vengeance.
> You had no hesitation   in guzzling your guests
> in your own home, so   Zeus and the gods have got you.

The blind giant picks up a huge rock and hurls it at the voice. The surge from its impact almost sinks Odysseus' boat; nonetheless, when they are further out to sea Odysseus calls once again, despite the remonstrances of his crew:

> If any mortal man   should ever ask you, Cyclops,
> who it was who   horribly fouled your eyeball,
> say it was Odysseus   taker of Troy who stopped your sight,
> Laertes' only son   who keeps his house on Ithaca.

Now Polyphemus utters the curse that will lead Poseidon to give Odysseus such a hard time over the next nine years:

> 'Earth-shaper Poseidon,   gloom-haired, hear me:
> if I'm surely your son   and you're fully my father,
> stop Troy-taker Odysseus   from ever arriving home.
> Or if it's fated for him   to reclaim his family,
> to reach his rich house   and his fatherland, then
> let it be late and hard,   with all his comrades dead,
> stowed on a ship not his,   to find havoc in his home.'
> This was the Cyclops' curse,   and the gloom-haired god heard
> > him.

It is often claimed that Odysseus' boast is a mistake, a failure of *metis*, since without the name Polyphemus would not have been able to curse him. But surely it would have been even worse for Odysseus *not* to have given his name. The aim of the epic hero – whether he is formed of the Achillean mould or the Odyssean – is to win glory, to be talked about and celebrated, to be a name. To go around under the pseudonym of Noman is a risky business: it is rather too close to being a nobody, an *outidanos* (like Dud Noman, the 'hero' of J. C. Powys' novel *Maiden Castle*). In order to claim the Cyclops episode as part of his own story, Odysseus needs to give it, so to speak, his signature.

His name and his fame will run into further dangers as his adventures go on, before he spends his seven lost years concealed on the island of Calypso. It is back from this state of near-anonymity that Odysseus has to win his way among the Phaeacians, before he can eventually make his declaration:

> I'm called Odysseus, son   of Laertes, so celebrated
> for tricks and deceit   that my glory reaches the skies.

He then reinforces his name by telling the story of his lost years. Storytelling restores this no one to being a someone.

TRIALS OF BODY AND SPIRIT
When Odysseus has finished, the Phaeacians

> . . . sat still in silence
> all through the twilit hall   enthralled by the spell of his story.

His stories still have that power; yet they are not just rattling good yarns. They were no doubt originally derived from sea tales, some of them told back in Mycenean times; like *Sinbad the Sailor* and others, such yarns are popular the world over. Yet there is, everyone feels, something more behind the stories of the *Odyssey*.

A favourite 'key' has been the belief that beneath these fantastic tales there lies a reality – real places, real voyages. Many thought this even in ancient times – that is why for example, the Aeolian islands off southern Italy, still called the Isole Eolie, got their name, as that is where Aeolus was supposed to have lived. Yet Homer explicitly says that Aeolus' island 'floated'. There were also ancient sceptics. Before 200 BC the geographer Eratosthenes said that, if someone could locate the cobbler who made the bag in which Aeolus put the winds, then he would believe the rest of his geographical identifications.

The Odysseus, spelled Olyseus, in this burlesque painting (the other side of the one shown on p. 106) travels on a raft of wine jars, blown by the north wind.

Undeterred by such disbelief, in modern times at least seventy different attempts have been made to reconstruct the geography of the *Odyssey*, some staying within the Mediterranean, others venturing out through the Pillars of Hercules (the Straits of Gibraltar), as far as Norway and South Africa. Take the Cimmerians:

> There the Cimmerians have settled their country and city
> all covered in cloud and mists, so that the sun's
> bright beams never penetrate through to them . . .
> a night-like gloom looms forever over these mortals.

Inevitably, someone has identified their land as Britain. That is at least more plausible than the theory of Gilbert Pillot who exclaimed of Calypso's balmy island: 'I believe in Iceland!'

The most ingeniously argued and probably the most influential identification was that of Victor Bérard, published in 1902. He claimed that Odysseus was originally a real Mycenean merchant-adventurer, but that for his voyages Homer followed a Phoenician log-book. The Phoenicians, Semitic people from the area of modern Lebanon, were indeed great travellers and voyagers throughout the Mediterranean in early times, and figure as such in the *Odyssey*.

Also at the turn of the century, the aged Samuel Butler was obsessed with placing his authoress of the *Odyssey* in Sicily, and was often to be seen there with his admiralty charts, maps and camera. Jane Harrison, a Greek scholar and one of the pioneers of education for women at Cambridge, remembered him 'badgering' her with his theories in the restaurant of an Athens hotel.

The *Odyssey* is too large and too resilient ever to yield to a single key. Yet it is characteristic of each of the 'geographers' to claim to have discovered for the first time the long-lost secret of the *Odyssey*. They speak of the 'initiated' and of 'treasure hunts'. Pillot's book, called *The Secret Code of the Odyssey*, is subtitled *Did the Greeks ever sail the Atlantic?* The latest in this line is Tim Severin. After sailing a leather boat across the Atlantic in the wake of St Brendan, he took his good ship *Argo* in the wake of Odysseus in 1985. Ironically, he concluded by locating nearly all the voyages in the vicinity of Ithaca. The *Argo* is a reconstruction of a Bronze Age galley, and Severin's claim was that no one had really tried their hand at Bronze Age navigation since before 1000 BC. This is true – and not least of Homer, as well as of the oral poets in the centuries between him and the Bronze Age. We believe that the 'reality' that underlies the wanderings is the reality of poetry, not of maritime engineering and geography.

But if the *Odyssey* is not 'true', does that make it false, all lies? This was the complaint of Plato who banished Homer from his ideal state. An ancient defence against Plato and earlier detractors was to treat Homer as allegory; that is, as a story with a deeper 'truer' meaning. One who held this view, Heraclitus, writing in the first century AD, even said 'Let Plato the parasite, the traducer of Homer, be banished.' According to him, the Lotus-eaters represented the temptations of gourmet food, the Cyclops of savage anger, Circe of exotic

A Circe *to outdo those of Hollywood, painted by Wright Barker in about 1900.*

vices, and so forth. The visit to the Underworld shows the depths to which intelligence will go to find knowledge.

The Stoics saw the endurance of Odysseus as a model for their philosophy, in contrast with Virgil and other Roman writers who took the Trojan side. 'Why bother with the literal geography of his journeys?' asked Seneca in the first century AD, 'when each day we encounter our own storms, and are driven by vice into every one of the troubles that Ulysses knew.'

Even some early Christian Fathers were prepared to find the voice of their true God in Homer. In St Ambrose's interpretation of the Sirens, the mast to which Odysseus was bound is the cross to which Christians must bind themselves when they are tempted by the lure of worldly pleasures. Other pious interpreters writing much later were even more far-fetched: for them the olive stake in the Cyclops story represented the cross, and Odysseus' wine the sacrament. In Spain, the seventeenth-century playwright Caldéron put on a Christian allegorical play, *The Charms of Sin*, in which Circe's speeches have been described as 'voluptuous hymns to sensual pleasure'. The culmination of these moralising interpretations of Homer came with François de Salignac de la Mothe Fénelon's romance *Télémaque*, written for the son of the Dauphin in 1699, and all the rage throughout Europe. This is the story of Telemachus, modelled on that of Odysseus, and oozing with exemplars of virtuous behaviour.

It is not hard to see why Robert Wood and the Romantic Age rejected such 'extravagant fancies'. For them the *Odyssey* was too real to be reduced to a sermon in deep sea sailor's dress, and did not need to be piously excused.

At the same time, there surely is both an inner and an outer journey in the *Odyssey*. Odysseus is undergoing trials of the spirit as well as strenuous physical adventures. His curiosity – his Captain Kirk spirit – gains him experience. He could not possibly refuse to listen to the song of the Sirens:

In this little-known picture painted in Athens in the fifth century BC, the half-woman half-bird Siren plays a musical instrument to Odysseus who is bound to the mast of his ship.

OPPOSITE] *Fuseli's vision,
unpredictable as ever, of
Odysseus between Scylla and
Charybdis.*

This way, come ashore,   celebrated Odysseus
far-famed Achaean,   come hear our music.
Nobody's ever sped by   in his ship without first
hearing the harmony   that pours from our lips.
He sails on his way   a wiser and happier man.
We know all the stories   of the exploits at Troy,
where you Greeks struggled   because the gods wanted it.
We know every event   throughout the fruitful earth.

Yet, by putting wax in his sailors' ears and having himself tied to the mast, Odysseus survives their lure.

Wherever he goes, whatever the danger, he always wants to know what kind of society he has arrived at. All the time he is gaining experience to help him to face and cope with whatever he may encounter later. Above all, he learns about lawlessness, anarchy and perversions of civilised behaviour. There is a wonderful reminder of this at a most unexpected moment, just before the end of his story. Odysseus, now all by himself, is hanging by his hands from a fig tree over the sea, waiting for the whirlpool of Charybdis:

I clung onto the trunk   grimly, until she should spew
the mast and timbers back.   Long I longed, till at last
at about the hour a man,   who has spent the day in the city
deciding the disputes   between young litigants,
gets up to go home   to his supper – about that hour
of dusk, those planks   came back up from Charybdis.

The world of order and civic duty is juxtaposed with the fantastic ordeals.

The monsters may be weird, but that does not deprive Odysseus' confrontations with them of a human meaning. This is the point that George Seferis makes in his poem *Reflections on a foreign line of verse*:

The superhuman one-eyed Cyclops, the Sirens who make you
    forget with their song, Scylla and Charybdis:
So many complex monsters that prevent us from remembering
    that he too was a man struggling in the world with a
    soul and body.

Not least, Odysseus gains experience in keeping his wits about him and in biding his time. This will be crucial to his success on Ithaca. In the Cyclops' cave he resisted the urge to kill Polyphemus at the first opportunity. Again and again on Ithaca he does not reveal himself and does not take action too soon. Before he even reaches his palace he has an encounter with the suitors' servant Melanthius at the fountain of Ithaca. Melanthius abuses the man whom he takes to be a wandering beggar, and tries to kick him into the ditch:

As he passed he stupidly   kicked him hard on the hip,
and yet he didn't   knock him off the trackway.
Odysseus stood his ground   and wondered whether
to flail the life from him   with his stick, or to take him

round the middle and   crack his skull on the rocks.
Yet he put up with it,   and held it all inside him.

The 'spiritual' dimension of the wanderings never dominates or dictates the narrative. The reality of the adventure carries the story along with its spellbinding momentum. So, too, although many of the incidents are fantastic and many of the locations quite unlike anything in the known world, there is always a solidity about them. Compared with such stories the world over, the *Odyssey* is remarkably free from the bizarre and the miraculous: Odysseus does not fly, or have a magic lamp, or talk to garrulous sea-birds. There are also always touches of homely detail – Polyphemus' cheese-making equipment, for example, or the fig tree on the cliff above Charybdis – touches which anchor the wanderings in a believable world. Indeed, it is these which have lured Tim Severin and so many before him on their own wanderings. Those who reject attempts to site the *Odyssey* in the actual world, on the other hand, often speak of Odysseus' adventures as set 'in fairyland'. But surely that is the wrong word: it is the tangible world of the audience's own experience transformed, as ever, by Homer's imagination.

When Henri Matisse was commissioned to illustrate an edition of James Joyce's Ulysses *in 1935, he in fact illustrated the* Odyssey – *here the blinding of Polyphemus.*

THE ONE-EYED GIANT IN DUBLIN

The expanded horizons of the twentieth century have broadened the locations for the wanderings of Odysseus in his various modern guises. The Greek poet Nikos Kazantzakis, in his monumental poem *The Odyssey: A Modern Sequel*, takes his hero through Crete, Egypt and Africa to Antarctica. The voyagers of Arthur C. Clarke's *2001 A Space Odyssey* are sent deep into the unexplored reaches of the solar system.

Paradoxically, the most creative modern conception contracts the wanderings to a rough square mile of Dublin on a single day, 16 June 1904. Leopold Bloom, a 38-year-old advertising salesman, visits a public bath, a cemetery, a newspaper office, a library, a public house, a maternity hospital and a brothel. When *Ulysses* was originally published serially in *The Little Review*, Joyce headed each episode with the title of its Homeric parallel, *Sirens*, *Nausicaa* and so on. But these do not appear in the book, and the relationship of *Ulysses* with its prototype has always been an issue.

There has been an especially lively debate on whether the contracted stage on which Joyce places his *dramatis personae*, above all his Odysseus, implies reduced stature. Ezra Pound, for example, argued that Joyce was merely using Homer to give some shape to a relatively plotless work; others have seen Bloom as representative of the littleness of modern life in contrast with the heroic past. But, while the correspondences with the *Odyssey* vary enormously – and are often very witty – Joyce's use of Homer was far more integral to his work than some kind of academic game. (The links are close, but Henri Matisse went too far. When asked why his illustrations for a special edition had so little bearing on Joyce's *Ulysses*, he replied: 'Je ne l'ai pas lu'. He had illustrated Homer!)

Joyce studied the *Odyssey* with care and attempted a Homeric fusion of reality and myth. He also drew on his wide-ranging secondary reading. For example, he was attracted by an etymology of the name Odysseus that alleged that it came from Outis-Zeus a combination of Noman and the king of the gods. His Ulysses was to be a god and a nobody. Bérard's theory about the Semitic origins of the *Odyssey* provided a synthesis for this growing conception. As Richard Ellmann, Joyce's biographer, observed: 'Joyce needed to find a pagan hero whom he could set loose in a Catholic city to make Ulysses a Dubliner.'

His Ulysses would be a Jew. As his name Leopold Bloom suggests, he would be the archetype of the insignificant immigrant, yet nonetheless possessing characteristics that overlapped with those of Odysseus. 'Look at them,' Joyce commented to Frank Budgen, 'they are better husbands than we are, better fathers and better sons.' But he could also represent the wider emblem of the Wandering Jew – an alternative manifestation of Odysseus. While entirely believable and lovable, Bloom is a composite reflection of Joyce's phenomenal memory and eclectic reading: 'He's an allroundman, Bloom is . . .'

As Odysseus, and more than Odysseus, his encounter with the

An old photo of Barney Kiernan's bar, setting of Leopold Bloom's encounter with the Dublin Cyclops.

Dublin Cyclops – as terrifying in his own way as Polyphemus – brings out and tests the more godlike aspect of this 'nobody'. It is four o'clock, and Bloom has agreed to meet two friends outside the Green Street Courthouse. When they do not appear he pops into Barney Kiernan's pub in Little Britain Street. There sits the unnamed 'citizen', drinking round after round of Guinness with the various regulars. He is described in 'epic' language:

> From shoulder to shoulder he measured several ells and his rock-like mountainous knees were covered . . . with a strong growth of tawny prickly hair. . . . The widewinged nostrils . . . were of such capaciousness that within their cavernous obscurity the fieldlark might easily have lodged her nest.

These proportions reflect his need to dominate the company, in keeping with his other Cyclopean characteristic, narrow vision. The citizen is an Irish Nationalist whose fanaticism leads him to appropriate Patrick W. Shakespeare, Thomas Cook and Son and the Queen of Sheba to his cause.

In the discussion that follows, Bloom stands up to his one-eyed adversary by insisting upon seeing every question from both sides.

When the others praise Gaelic sports for 'building up a nation again', Bloom speaks out in favour of a more gentle game: 'What I meant about tennis, for example, is the agility and training the eye.' References to eyes and blindness accumulate ('The Nelson Policy', for example) as the citizen's nationalism is exposed as thin cover for his xenophobia:

> Those are nice things, says the citizen, coming over here to Ireland filling the country with bugs. . . . Swindling the peasants, says the citizen, and the poor of Ireland. We want no more strangers in our house.

As a pacifist, Bloom stands up to the citizen with words. While he is speaking he almost burns himself on his smouldering cigar butt, a sort of reversal of Odysseus preparing to blind Polyphemus. Still, his bravery in the face of brute force ennobles the scene, and another allusion to Odysseus' olive-wood stake associates him with an even more exalted personage: 'Some people can see the mote in others eyes but they can't see the beam in their own.' His blinding defiance of the citizen has similar undertones:

> – But it's no use, says he. Force, hatred, history, all that. That's not life for men and women, insult and hatred. And everybody knows that it's the very opposite of that that is really life.
> – What? says Alf.
> Love, says Bloom. I mean the opposite of hatred. I must go now.

As his friends hurry him out, the citizen jeers 'three cheers for Israel!'. Odysseus with his Noman trick is in danger of losing his name. Bloom's name (already caricatured as Herr Professor Luitpold Blumenduft) is in fact a kind of concealment: when he came to Ireland from Hungary his father changed it from Viraj – the Hungarian for flower. As he makes his escape Viraj/Odysseus now risks everything by declaring himself:

> – Mendelssohn was a jew and Karl Marx and Mercadante and Spinoza. And the saviour was a jew and his father was a jew. Your God.
> – He had no father, says Martin. That'll do now. Drive ahead.
> – Whose God? says the citizen.
> – Well, his uncle was a jew, says he. Your God was a jew. Christ was a jew like me.
> Gob, the citizen made a plunge back into the shop.
> – By Jesus, says he, I'll brain that bloody jewman for using the holy name. By Jesus, I'll crucify him so I will. Give us that biscuitbox here.

The sun is in the citizen's eyes ('Where is he till I murder him?') and the Jacob's biscuit tin – Polyphemus' rock – misses its target. The episode culminates with the epic carriage ascending to heaven. Yet its last word brings the apotheosised Noman down to earth:

And they beheld Him even Him, ben Bloom Elijah, amid clouds of angels ascend to the glory of the brightness at an angle of fortyfive degrees over Donohoe's in Little Green Street like a shot off a shovel.

As an exile from the earth of Dublin and of Ireland, Joyce took immense pains to create an accurate picture of the place at a specific time in 1904. He used maps, timetables and books; he told Budgen: 'I want to give a picture of Dublin so complete that if the city one day disappeared from the earth it could be reconstructed out of my

O'Connell Bridge in the heart of Dublin in about 1904, with Nelson's Column in the distance.

book.' There is, for example, a precise topical reference when the citizen provocatively invokes 'Sinn Fein!'. This was the official title of the patriotic movement when it became a political party the following year in 1905. Some of Joyce's locations have, however, felt the effect of Irish Republicanism more than Joyce could ever have foreseen. The Green Street Courthouse is now the Special Criminal Court, where many IRA suspects have been tried. The IRA may well also have been responsible for the bomb which expertly removed the top half of Nelson's Pillar – a central Dublin landmark – in 1966. Barney Kiernan's pub is now a unisex hair salon called *As You Like It*. And the town planners have gone further in defacing Joyce's Dublin: 7 Eccles Street was demolished to make way for a private hospital in 1982 – though individual bricks and other relics are scattered throughout the literate world.

Yet, untouched by two world wars, the city remains largely unchanged; and every bookshop sells annotated itineraries to help tourists trace, step by step and hour by hour, the journey of Leopold Bloom. At the same time, Joyce's *Odyssey* is far more than a paper itinerary, as it is more than *Thom's Official Directory* which he constantly consulted.

ROUNDED WITH A SLEEP

In Homer, the last of Odysseus' adventures abroad – his experiences with the Phaeacians on Scherie – is told by the poet direct. Though the account of Scherie may contain elements of the real Corfu, it still does not belong to the 'real' world of geography, not even in the sense that Troy and Cape Maleia and Ithaca are 'real'. But it is a kind of model of a civilised and well-ordered society. Odysseus is treated with courtesy, and Alcinous proposes generous guest-gifts. He and the twelve leading Phaeacians give him a bronze tripod-cauldron each, as well as gold and fine cloth, as he sets off for Ithaca. The half-way world of the Phaeacians is most apparent in their seafaring. They are great seamen, yet they do not trade; indeed, their only purpose seems to be to take wanderers home. King Alcinous says to Odysseus:

> Tell me your homeland,   your city and its country,
> so our ships may transport   you there, calculating their course.
> For we Phaeacians   have no place for pilots,
> no use for rudders,   such as steer all common craft;
> the ships themselves   can sense the thoughts of men,
> and with their own minds   know all towns and fertile plains
> over the salt ocean;   invisible in mist,
> they fly fast, without fear   of trouble, attack or wreck.

This helps to account for something strange about the journey they make with Odysseus – they take him back by night. In ancient Greece it was normal to sail by day and to camp on shore overnight. Seafaring was dangerous. As one of Odysseus' sailors says:

LL BRIDGE. DUBLIN. 1704. W. !.

This double-page spread from an American comic-strip version of the entire Odyssey *covers the division between the two halves.*

Tricky winds suddenly   spring up at night, destroyers of ships.

Yet when Alcinous first promises Odysseus his passage home he says:

> During the voyage you   can lie lost deep in sleep,
> while they row over   the calm depth until they come
> to your house and homeland   or wherever else you will.

Queen Arete says:

> As you lie in sweet sleep   on board the dark boat.

From then on, it is taken for granted that Odysseus will depart at nightfall. On his last day on Scherie, Demodocus sings once more. The opportunity to hear and to tell his own story has been important for Odysseus, but now he has lost interest in the bard:

> Often he turned his face   towards the shining sun,
> keen to see it set   and aching to weigh anchor.

The time eventually comes to turn to action, and so to provide future poets with more of his story. He makes a simple but touching farewell and then:

When they'd walked down   to the ship moored by the shore,
Odysseus' escort   took over the treasure,
supplies and wine,   and stowed them in the boat.
For Odysseus they spread   a blanket on deck
and linen at the stern,   so he could sleep sound.
He himself embarked   and lay straight down on deck
without one word.   Each man on the benches
sat in his proper place;   the rope was slipped from its stone.
They all leant to the oar   throwing spray with their blades,
while a sweet sleep   descended on his lids,
wonderful, unwakeable,   next door to death.
The ship, as a four-horse   team streams over the level,
all four careering off   under the crack of the lash,
rearing their hooves high,   quickly cover the track,
so the prow rode high,   and in their wake the wave
of the rushing ocean   seethed in a deep blue path.
So she swept on   unfaltering – even the falcon,
the quickest of hawks,   could not have kept pace.
She slipped onwards   cutting through the water,
transporting that man,   whose mind rivalled the gods,
who had borne before   all sorts of trials and troubles,
both in battles on land   and crossing the stressful sea.
But now he slept in peace,   forgetful of all past pain.

This sleep does not merely mark the passage from Corfu to Ithaca, a mundane trip made every year by hundreds of tourists. It is a transition between worlds, a return through an almost deathlike sleep from a dream life to a real life. And these are the final lines of the first of the two great sessions sung by the bard Homer.

6 ITHACA IN DISGUISE

I have some idea of purchasing the island of Ithaca

Byron

Part two of the *Odyssey* begins:

About the hour   when that brightest star rises,
which shines to announce   the first flush of dawn,
the ship from over the sea   arrived at the island.
In the country of Ithaca   is the cove of Phorcys,
the ancient god of the ocean.   There is a pair of promontories
sheer towards the ocean   but sheltering the inlet;
these keep out the breakers   raised by the roaring storms
at sea, and inside   the timbers of ships can rest
in unanchored calm   at the end of their journey.
At the harbour-head   is a leafy olive tree,
and close to it a cave,   half-lit and lovely,
held as sacred to   the nymphs called Naiads.
Within the cavern   there are jugs and jars
shaped in stone where   honey-bees have built their hives:
and long looms are hung   in stone there, where the nymphs
weave crimson cloths,   an astonishing sight –
and ever-running water.   Two openings enter:
the one towards the north   must be used by humans;
the way facing south   is divine, and is not
taken by mankind   – the gods go through that one.
This inlet was well-known   to the Phaeacian sailors,
who rowed so strongly   that they drove their boat on the beach
to half its whole length.   Then they disembarked,
and first they lifted down   Odysseus from the deck,
blanket and linen   and all wrapped about him,
and set him down on the sand   still deeply asleep,
and unloaded all   the possessions which the princes,
thanks to Athene,   had offered him as he left.
These they piled in a heap   by the trunk of the olive tree,
well off the pathway,   in case any travelling man
should steal Odysseus' treasure   while he still slept.

No one on Ithaca ever sees the Phaeacians, not even Odysseus
himself. Because he is not aware of disembarking from their boat, but
is deposited on land fast asleep, his arrival has a strangely unreal

126

feeling. He is not landed at the port but at a more remote spot, the harbour sacred to the sea god Phorcys. As it is crucial to the plot that no one should have warning that Odysseus has returned, this is just as well.

When Odysseus awakes, Athena distorts his perception of the place so that he does not at first recognise the landscape. The scene which ensues between Odysseus and his patron goddess is subtle and entertaining; it was fully exploited by Monteverdi in his opera *Il Ritorno d'Ulisse in Patria* (1641), which follows the *Odyssey* closely. Athena first appears to him in the form of a noble young shepherd and tells him that the place is Ithaca. Instead of responding openly, he spins her an elaborate yarn about how he is a fugitive from Crete.

> He spoke. She smiled,   the glinting-eyed goddess Athena,
> caressing him softly . . . she winged him these words:
> 'It would need someone   of incredible craft and crookedness
> to outstrip you in deceit   – even against a god –
> such subtle cunning,   so stuffed full of tricks!
> Not even in your own land   will you drop your deceit,
> or stop twisting the truth   – you're tricky from top to toe.'

It is this very skill at lying that Athena is so fond of. Only now does she enable him to recognise his own country:

> 'Now I'll show you the shape   of Ithaca – that will convince you.
> This is the cove of Phorcys,   the ancient god of the ocean,
> and at the harbour-head   is as ever the leafy olive,
> and here is the huge wide   cavern where in the old days
> with full ritual you offered   sacrifice to the Nymphs,
> and here swathed with woods   is the mountain of Neritos.'
> The goddess dispersed   the mist and the landscape emerged.
> Then Odysseus the endurer   was filled with delight;
> glad in his own land   he kissed the grain-giving ground,
> and lifting his hands on high   he formed a prayer to the
>   Nymphs:
> 'My Naiad Nymphs,   dear daughters of Zeus, I never
> supposed I would see you   again. Now glad greetings . . .'

James Joyce's metamorphosis of this scene is to have Leopold Bloom kiss the microcosm of his own private world – Molly's buttocks:

> – He kissed the plump mellow yellow smellow melons of her rump, on each plump melonous hemisphere, in their mellow yellow furrow with obscure prolonged provocative melon smellonous osculation.

Athena tells Odysseus about the suitors, and he responds:

> I could, I can see,   have met with the doom of Agamemnon
> in my own home,   a bad end, had you not, goddess,
> told me the whole   situation point by point.
> Now let's spin cunningly   to pay them back completely.

An engraving of one of the scenes painted by Primaticcio for the 'Galerie D'Ulysse' at Fontainebleau, completed in 1570, but now destroyed. Once Athena clears the mist, Odysseus recognises and kisses the land of Ithaca. On the left is a preview of the scene at Eumaeus' farm.

With her help he will avoid the fate of Agamemnon, who returned triumphant from Troy only to be slaughtered by his own wife Clytemnestra and her lover Aegisthus.

THE DOG ON THE THRESHOLD

Athena now transforms Odysseus' physique and clothing so that he has the appearance of an old man in rags. She advises him to go first to the house of his pig-farmer Eumaeus. At the end of the scene she goes off to fetch Odysseus' son Telemachus from Sparta, where the narrative left him many hours ago before it turned to Odysseus.

> Leaving the enclosed cove   Odysseus took the rough track
> over the high ground and through   the woods, the way Athena
> had shown, to the swineherd.   Of all Odysseus' household
> he was the one who cared   most for his master's goods.
> He came on him   sitting in front of the farmhouse,
> where he'd built his high   yard-wall in a sheltered spot.
> He'd made it himself,   a good large clearing
> to pen in the pigs   of his lord while he was absent . . .

128

Eumaeus is the first man that Odysseus meets on his return. He receives the ragged beggar with courtesy and provides him generously with food, shelter and conversation. Telemachus arrives. Only after Eumaeus has set off to the town to reassure Penelope of her son's safe return, does the father reveal himself to the young man he left behind as a baby:

> I'm not a god but your   father, for whose sake you've suffered
> so long in sorrow,   maltreated by other men.

Odysseus' plan is that Telemachus should go ahead next morning to the town, and that he himself will then set off towards evening, accompanied by Eumaeus. The time has come for Odysseus to face the dangers of his own home.

> Over his shoulder he slung   a ragged old beggar's bag,
> all full of holes   and hung on a tattered string,
> and Eumaeus found him   a comfortable old stick.
> So the two set off   leaving the dogs and the lads
> to look after the farm.   Eumaeus thus led his lord
> to the town, looking like a   vagrant old vagabond
> with a stick, and clothed   in rags and tatters.
> When their stony track   got close to the city,
> they approached the spring,   clear-flowing in its channel,
> which supplied the people   – it had been built by
> Neritos and   Polyctor and king Ithacus.
> Poplars had been planted   all round in a grove,
> trees that grow by water;   the cold stream cascades
> down from a stone, and above   an altar to the Nymphs . . .

This journey from Eumaeus' farm to the palace takes Odysseus from the rural but honest world of the fields and obscure peasants to the dangerous world of the town, where the suitors rampage. On the way, at the spring of Ithaca (a significant place, as at Troy) they meet Melanthius, the chief servant of the suitors – a sort of sinister counterpart to Eumaeus. His sister Melantho is the leader of the corrupt women servants in the palace, who sleep with the suitors. (Monteverdi takes up a hint in Homer and invents a saucy sub-plot between her and their villainous ring-leader Eurimaco.)

The savour of roasting meat and the sound of Phemius warming up on his lyre assail Odysseus even before he enters his palace, with its high walls surrounding a large open courtyard. In the courtyard, before he comes to the actual doorway of the hall, he is to be recognised for the first time by a living creature on Ithaca:

> There lay an animal,   which, lifting its head, pricked up
> its ears, the dog Argos –   Odysseus's old dog which he'd
> hand-reared himself,   but never had any benefit of him
> before he left for Troy.   In the old days the young bloods
> used to take him with them   hunting hares, wild goats and deer.
> With his master away,   he'd become cast aside

> with his bed on the midden,   donkey and cattle dung
> piled in a great heap   in the yard before the doors,
> for Odysseus' servants   to fetch as manure for his farm.
> There lies old Argos,   all infested with fleas and lice.
> The dog recognised   Odysseus as he drew close;
> he wagged with his tail   and lowered both ears, only
> with no strength any longer   to move towards his master . . .

Odysseus realises that this must be Argos, but to maintain his disguise he cannot acknowledge him.

> As for Argos   the hand of dark death took him,
> once he'd seen Odysseus,   after twenty years away.

A few moments later Odysseus reaches the vital transition on his return home, the doorway of his own hall:

> Odysseus, close behind   Eumaeus, entered his own
> palace, looking just like   a vagrant old vagabond
> with a stick, and clothed   in rags and tatters.
> Inside the doors   he squatted on the threshold, against
> the cypress-wood door-post,   which once a craftsman
> had skilfully shaped   and smoothed true to a line.

'ENDURE, OLD HEART'

During the long evening, the suitors give more than enough evidence of their greed, discourtesy and wilful malice. Odysseus at last manages to have a long conversation with Penelope, but, again, he intricately weaves a false past for himself and conceals his identity. This time he claims to be the younger brother of the king of Crete, rich enough to have had servants and to have given lavish guest-gifts; but now fallen on hard times. He tells how twenty years earlier he saw Odysseus on his way to Troy, and describes in detail the clothes that he had on:

> I noticed too the tunic   that he was wearing:
> it shone like the skin   of a sun-dried onion,
> it was as soft as that,   and glowed like the sun's gleam.
> Many women   stood round and admired it.

Since Penelope had made these herself, she is completely taken in by the element of truth which is woven in among fictitious adventures.

In *Ulysses*, Leopold Bloom's day has consisted of mundane wanderings around the city of Dublin. Often his mind has been filled with the jingle of an advertisement:

> What is home without
> Plumtree's Potted Meat?
>   Incomplete.
> With it an abode of bliss.

In his imagination, however, he pictures himself in exotic locations redolent of the Arabian Nights:

Somewhere in the east: early morning: set off at dawn. . . .
Wander through awned streets. Turbaned faces going by. Dark
caves of carpet shops, big man, Turko the terrible, seated cross-
legged, smoking a coiled pipe. Cries of sellers in the street. Drink
water scented with fennel, sherbet . . . Getting on to sundown.
The shadows of the mosques among the pillars. . . . A mother
watches me from her doorway. She calls her children home in their
dark language. High walls: beyond strings twanged. Night sky,
moon, violet, colour of Molly's new garters.

Odysseus, who has, on the contrary, really undergone exotic
wanderings, offers fictitious adventures which are relatively everyday and plausible.

A second faithful old friend recognises who he really is that
evening – his nurse Eurycleia. She is given the task of washing the
vagabond's feet; and, once it is exposed, immediately knows the
deep scar just above his knee which he got from a boar's tusk when
hunting on Mount Parnassus as a young man. Odysseus stifles her
cry and binds her to secrecy.

At long last Odysseus settles down for his first night back in his
own house, in the forecourt, lying on an untanned ox-hide. Concealment is more essential than ever, whatever the provocation.

While he lay awake   Odysseus was laying his plots
against the suitors.   Then the women who used
to sleep with the suitors   came on their way through the hall,
making jokes and   giggling with each another.
His fury was roused   as he disputed in his spirit:
whether to jump up   and butcher them each and all,

*A cup painted in Athens in
about 440 BC, now in Chiusi,
showing the washing of the
'beggar' Odysseus.*

131

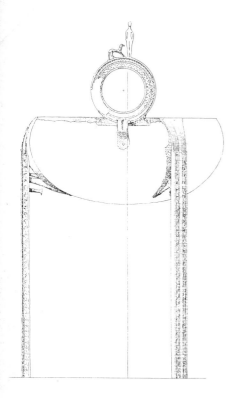

A drawing which reconstructs one of the tripods found in the Polis Bay 'cave' in the 1930s.

OPPOSITE ABOVE] *A view of Polis Bay from the north. The site of the Cave of the Nymphs is about two-thirds of the way from the headland towards the angle of the bay.*

OPPOSITE BELOW] *Polis Bay taken by the little landing-stage visible in the picture above. The 'cave' is just beyond the small headland on the right.*

or else to let them lie, to make love one last time
with the insolent suitors. His spleen growled inside.
As a dog growls in defence of her helpless pups
against a stranger, and isn't frightened to fight,
so his spleen growled as he witnessed this wickedness.
Striking his chest he reproached his spirit:
'Endure, old heart, you put up with worse than this
on the day that the cruel Cyclops crunched
my brave comrades; yet you endured then,
and your cunning contrived an escape from the cave of death.'
So he hectored his heart, and it stayed fast fastened,
and doggedly endured. Yet he twisted this way and that;
as a cook keeps turning a hot haggis filled with fat and blood
over a flaming fire, and is keen to see it all cooked,
so Odysseus twisted this way and that, as he thought
how to lay his hands on the shameless suitors,
one man among many . . .

TWO CAVES INTO ONE

The second great session of performance, according to our theory, begins with a detailed description, full of fresh particularity, of the sheltered gulf on Ithaca where Odysseus is landed. The remarkable natural harbour at Vathý fits Homer's description of the cove of Phorcys extraordinarily well.

Homer also lavishes details on the Cave of the Nymphs (quoted on page 126). After she has revealed the island to him, Athena helps Odysseus to hide his treasure here:

'First straight away we'll place all these possessions
inside the sacred cave where they'll stay secure.
Then we'll lay our plans to get the best outcome.'
With these words Athena went inside the twilight
of the cavern to look for hiding places; and Odysseus
went and fetched all the gold and resilient bronze
and fine-finished cloth which the Phaeacians had given him.
They stowed it well within, and then Pallas Athena,
daughter of strong Zeus, blocked the door with a boulder.
They sat together, backs to the trunk of the sacred
olive, to plot the end of the strutting suitors.

Homer's descriptions are so 'real' that, ever since its creation, people have been searching on Ithaca for the haven, its cave, and the other landmarks of the *Odyssey*. There is no doubt that the ancient Greeks thought they knew where the Cave of the Nymphs was. On the shore of Polis Bay, in the northwest of the island, about 20 kilometres from Vathý, there was a large cave whose roof collapsed, probably in the first century AD. It now looks like a very small cove. The site was first discovered in 1868 by the owner of the land, one Loizos. His earliest finds were bought by Heinrich Schliemann when he visited Ithaca. Loizos dug again at the site in 1873, and this time

*A bust of Odysseus looking out
to sea in the village of Stavros.
The inscription – 'A prayer
to Odysseus' – is taken from
the fragment found in the
nearby Cave of the Nymphs.*

found, among other things, a bronze tripod. We were told in the nearby village of Stavros that he had found a gold tripod, and – some added – a gold chicken that laid golden eggs. Local legend also tells that Loizos disappeared and that neither he nor his family have been heard of since.

In the 1930s the splendid English eccentric, Sylvia Benton, carried out proper excavations of the Polis Bay cave. These were made difficult by the constant inflow of sea water. She found ample evidence that there had been a cult of the Nymphs here. She also discovered a fragment of terracotta of the second century BC with neat letters inscribed on it saying: ΕΥΧΗΝ ΟΔΥΣΣΕΙ, 'A prayer to Odysseus', which suggests that in late classical times there was a hero-cult here. Hero-cults – the worship of the powerful dead below (as opposed to the immortal Olympian gods on high) – originally arose in Greece about the time of Homer, in the eighth or seventh century BC. They have some analogy with Christian worship of saints, and many churches in Greece stand on the sites of ancient sanctuaries. Some scholars connect the growth of these cults with the popularity of epic poetry. So Odysseus became a kind of pagan saint on Ithaca.

The cult of the Nymphs was by no means the only connection with the *Odyssey* that Benton discovered. Imagine her excitement when, chunk by water-logged chunk, she found the remains of twelve magnificent, three-legged cauldrons. These tripods, made of bronze and lavishly decorated, date from the ninth or eighth century BC. In the sand at that spot (which is not signposted for visitors) we were still able to find several tiny, bright green fragments of ancient bronze. In the museum of Stavros, where the dedicatory fragment to Odysseus is on show, we were allowed to pick up the leg of one of Benton's tripods: about 90 cm long and 5 cm by 2.5 cm thick, it was extremely heavy.

Odysseus hid the thirteen tripods which he was given on Scherie in the Cave of the Nymphs. Loizos found one tripod and Benton twelve. Yet they date from about 300 years after the Mycenean Age – possibly 100 years or so before Homer. Were the tripods placed there in the ninth century because the details of the story already existed? Not necessarily. We find it just as plausible to suppose that the tripods were dedicated one by one to the Nymphs, independently of the *Odyssey*. Then, if Homer visited the island in the eighth or seventh century, he would have seen them. This might well have given him the idea of having Odysseus hide his treasure as he does. (Is it a deliberate loose end in the *Odyssey* that Odysseus never goes back to collect it?)

Given the westward expansion of colonisers from Greece in the eighth century, it is not at all absurd to suppose that Homer had visited Ithaca. There are other features of the island, besides the harbour of Vathý and the Polis Bay cave, which may well have fed his imagination. For example, Athena gives Odysseus details of the whereabouts of Eumaeus:

The pigs are gathered   by Crow Crag and Arethusa spring,
crunching nourishing acorns   and drinking the dark pond.

In the southeast corner of the island there is an impressive cliff with a
good spring beneath it. Local peasants, eager to please, will even tell
visitors that it is called 'Crow's Crag'.

And there is another cave. This one is confidently signposted for
tourists: 'To the Cave of the Nymphs' (it is called Marmarospilia in
Greek), and is about half an hour's bumpy scooter ride out of Vathý.
From outside there is a magnificent view of the central gulf of Ithaca.
You enter through a small north-facing fissure in the hillside, and
climb down some perilous old iron steps to arrive in a huge, roughly
circular cavern with strangely shaped stone formations dripping
with water. It is not completely dark because light filters in through a
small inaccessible opening way up in the roof. At midday, for about
an hour, a shaft of brilliant sunlight penetrates through this
'entrance of the gods', throwing a slowly moving circle of light onto
the floor of the cave.

ABOVE] *The 'human' entrance
at Marmorospilia. The
condition of the iron gate is
much the same as that of the
steep stairs inside. The
'entrance of the gods' is a little
further up the hillside.*

RIGHT] *The inside of
Marmarospilia, with the
'entrance of the gods' clearly
visible. Artificial lighting has
been used.*

To all appearances this is the Cave of the Nymphs as described in the opening verses of the second part of the *Odyssey*; but in the excited desire to give historical and geographical accuracy to Homer's story, two awkward facts have been generally suppressed. First, this cave is about 2 kilometres from the sea, and further than that from the haven of Vathý. Secondly, it is 200 metres above sea level. Yet Homer makes it quite clear that the Cave of the Nymphs is right by the shore, not an hour's strenuous scramble up the mountainside. It is quite a slog even on a motor-scooter. If Odysseus had to carry his thirteen tripods, along with his gold and other gifts, all the way up here, it would have taken him a week; and after that he would have been far too exhausted to confront the suitors.

This is the 'Pınarbaşı technique' once again. Homer has taken places which are separate in reality, and has fused and transformed them to accommodate his story. Reality is absorbed and re-emerges as poetry.

Some other details in the *Odyssey* do not fit so well. Two in particular are a nuisance for the 'verificationists'. The suitors lay a sea-ambush for Telemachus on the island of Asteris, between Ithaca and Same, modern Kefallinia. Asteris is described as small, but with two good harbours and windy lookout points. The only island between Ithaca and Kefallinia is tiny, low and harbourless. Secondly, Odysseus describes Ithaca to the Phaeacians like this:

> . . . an isle   which stands clear in the sun
> with the quivering woods   of its mountain Neritos.
> Several other islands   cluster around about,
> Zacynthos and its woods,   and Doulichion and Same.
> Ithaca's lower lying   and furthest towards the sunset.

Ithaca, however, is mountainous, not low, and is not the furthest to the west of its cluster of islands. This has led defenders to desperate straits, including the theory, which has raised even worse problems, that Homer's Ithaca was in reality Lévkas to the north.

No wonder that others have reacted, as Bryant did at Troy, against this whole approach. They say that, on the contrary, Homer had never been anywhere near Ithaca and had only heard vague reports of the islands, or even made up his various descriptions and landmarks entirely. Certainly, some of the Homeric identifications alleged over the centuries have been entirely spurious; for example, the Kastro (castle) of Odysseus on top of Mount Aetos. The *Odyssey* makes it perfectly clear that Odysseus' house does not stand apart on an acropolis but is within the town; these fortifications have, in any case, proved to date from the fifth century BC.

Faced with fictions of this sort, it is hard not to sympathise with the sentiments of Byron when a companion tried to drag him off on a tour of the Odyssean monuments. Byron retorted: 'Do I look like one of those emasculated fogeys? Let's have a swim. I detest antiquarian twaddle.' Once again, as at Troy, the answer seems to us to avoid the two extreme positions of the verificationists and the fictionalists:

OPPOSITE ABOVE] *The smaller conical mountain on the right is Mount Aetos, traditionally 'the castle of Odysseus'. And the archaeological site is on the slope to the right (north) of the road which passes over the saddle. The Gulf of Molo reaches in to make this narrow isthmus in the centre of the island.*

OPPOSITE BELOW] *The south slope of Mount Aetos, now established as the site of the main town of ancient Ithaca.*

great poetry is inspired by places and does not simply reproduce them.

NEW DIGS ON ITHACA

What, then, was Ithaca like in 700 or 650 BC when Homer might have been there? In particular, was there somewhere which could have fed Homer's imagination when he built up his picture of the city of Ithaca, quite a large place which includes the great house of Odysseus himself? Until recently there has been merely some evidence of the use of Ithaca, like Corfu, as a trading post on the newly opened shipping routes to the west, and none of a city or even a small town in this period. In four seasons of excavation since 1986, however, Professor Sarantis Symeonoglou of Washington University, Saint Louis, has organised the beginnings of an ambitious project to excavate the entire central saddle of the island. He has already established that the main town of ancient times was on this isthmus, beneath the acropolis of Mount Aietos. This is an area of about 800 square metres. Sylvia Benton did some excavation here in the 1930s, but even so, only a tiny percentage of the whole area has as yet been excavated.

This site offered its inhabitants water from wells, some relatively flat land, and safe control of the two harbours below. Constant rebuilding in antiquity, the natural erosion of the centuries, and the construction of olive terraces in more recent times have made excavation difficult and have severely damaged the ancient remains. Symeonoglou has found pottery dating back to the Bronze Age, and evidence of continued habitation through to the time of Christ when the site was abandoned. It seems that the people living here did not suffer too badly at the end of the Mycenean period and continued as a lively community even in the Dark Ages. Present evidence suggests that there was a small town of a few hundred people there in Homer's day, about as many as this slope could accommodate.

In a trial trench Symeonoglou has uncovered a portion of an eighth-century house with pottery, cooking utensils and even some pig bones. After exploring the site, the three of us shared a delicious meal of spit-roast sucking-pig down in Vathý, and thought of the suitors. Apart from domestic buildings, Symeonoglou has followed up excavations of a shrine found by the British team in the 1930s, and has gathered further evidence of a small temple with offerings ranging from the tenth to the sixth centuries BC. He believes that this was a temple to Apollo, and has recently acquired the site of the remains of a chapel to Saint George on the land, in the hope that this will produce more evidence. It would certainly fit well if Apollo is found to have had a special cult on Ithaca, since it is on a festival to the archer-god that Odysseus kills the suitors.

COUNTRY HOSPITALITY

Much of the second half of the *Odyssey* is set not in the town but far off along rough trackways in the outlying hills of Ithaca. Most of

three books – over two hours in performance – take place in
Eumaeus' farmhouse, and attention is lavished on humble, non-
heroic details; the kind of everyday touch that comes in the *Iliad* only
in the contrasting peacetime world of the similes. For example:

> He had made himself   a good large clearing
> to pen in the pigs   of his lord while he was absent,
> walled with quarried rock   and topped with wild pear branches;
> all round the outside   he ran a thick barricade
> of stakes made by splitting   the trunks of dark oak trees.

These techniques of husbandry can still be seen in rural Greece
today. When Eumaeus takes Odysseus into the house:

> Indoors he sat him down   on a heaped-up brushwood seat
> overspread with the skin   of a shaggy-coated goat,
> his own bedspread . . .

Through such homely details, particularly the meals that Eumaeus
prepares for Odysseus, Homer captures the honesty and the
generous hospitality of the poor countryman – something else still
found in Greece today.

On the day that we took the fishing boat to Cape Maleia we arrived
back at the harbour of Velanidhia at about eleven o'clock. Panayiotis'
wife Kyriaki came down to meet the boat. She filled a bucket with all
the fish they would be unable to sell: flat grey ones with hideous
whiskers, long thin ones with tiny sharp teeth, undersized mullet,
and crimson monsters that consisted almost entirely of head. They
took us up to their one-room cottage above the harbour, and Kyriaki
laid a red rag-rug and pillows under a carob tree in case we wanted to
sleep after our early start. By one o'clock she had created, with the
addition of lemon and olive oil, a delicious fish stew. Under an olive
tree at the side of the house they gathered planks and logs to impro-
vise an earth-level dining-room. We tucked in to bowls of yellow
stew, hunks of dry bread and giant, sweet spring onions. Iannis
poured glass after glass of his own home-grown wine – 100 per cent
natural, he proudly told us – until the two-litre bottle was empty.

For two English travellers who have never found that the niceties
of table manners come naturally, the meal had added attractions:
fishbones were spat or thrown into the undergrowth, fingers became
greasy, arms stretched across neighbours to reach a glass or spoon,
and bread was repeatedly dunked into the pot. Sun and wine soon
had everyone lolling on their stools or sprawled on the ground. Yet
our hosts were far from lacking in courtesy: our glasses were never
empty, our bowls constantly refilled with the choicest fish and roe.
When finally we had to leave, Kyriaki brought a tin jug of water and
clean hand towels out of the house. We felt honoured.

Our meal at Velanidhia was enlivened with storytelling of seafaring, piracy and treasure. There were occasional disputes about
whether some particular tale was myth or history. In the *Odyssey*
Odysseus entertains Eumaeus with stories, but the audience knows

*The fish are extracted from the
net and sorted, off Cape
Maleia. The unsellable fish
become that day's feast.*

that, plausible though they are, they are entirely fictitious. He mentions Crete, Egypt and Phoenicia; piracy, fabulous wealth and utter destitution; he even slips in a chance encounter with Odysseus and guarantees that he is on his way home. Eumaeus happily believes everything, except that his master will ever return. Disguise and storytelling are once again vital for Odysseus.

HIDDEN FEELINGS
The homely world of Eumaeus prepares for and contrasts with the dangerous world of the suitors inside the palace – disruptive, extravagant and contemptuous of courtesy and hospitality. Amidst all that corruption and treachery Odysseus can trust no one and must keep his identity hidden at all costs. From the time of his return to the palace until his self-revelation to the suitors ('Dogs, you were so damned sure   I'd never come home from Troy'), he is revealed only to Argos and Eurycleia – both times involuntarily – and, deliberately, to Eumaeus and the loyal cattle-herdsman Philoetius. Even when his own son Telemachus first enters Eumaeus' house, Odysseus shows no trace of personal response: instead, true to his role as the old beggar, he makes as if to give up his brushwood seat to the young master. Only after Eumaeus has gone, does he reveal his feelings:

So he kissed his son;   tears trickled down his cheeks
falling – though up till now   he'd remained unmoved.

Again and again, Odysseus plays the role of the old beggar with all the assurance and attention to detail of a great actor – or a bard. His most virtuoso performance is with Penelope; and it is with Penelope that he has to work hardest to conceal his emotions. When he spins her his particularly convincing story about how he saw Odysseus years ago in Crete, she weeps piteously like the thawing snow:

. . . her tears   melted the charm of her cheeks.
She mourned for her man,   even as he sat beside her.
Odysseus inside   pitied his wife as she wept,
but his eyes still stared,   as unswerving as iron or ivory,
lids unblinking.   Deceit concealed his tears.

Why should Odysseus treat Penelope with this distrust when there is such complete evidence of her loyalty and discretion? At least part of the answer lies in the cautionary tale of Agamemnon's return home from Troy.

Stories were told of the homecomings of other Greek heroes, and there was even an epic called *Nostoi*, 'The Returns'. These other *Nostoi* are alluded to here and there in the *Odyssey*; and in particular Menelaus recounts to Telemachus the story of his own return with Helen. But the homecoming which is recalled again and again is Agamemnon's murderous betrayal by Clytemnestra. Agamemnon's ghost in the Underworld tells Odysseus the whole sorry story, and concludes by warning him:

Another engraving from the lost series by Primaticcio (see p. 128), this shows the slaughter of Agamemnon and his comrades as recounted to Odysseus by Agamemnon's ghost. Agamemnon and his Trojan concubine Cassandra are being butchered in the foreground.

So you shouldn't be   too trustful of your wife.
Don't tell all the story,   however well worked out;
repeat part of it   and hold the rest hidden.
Not that your wife would   slaughter you – no danger,

Odysseus,

of that from one so wise   and sensible as Penelope.
She was a fresh young wife   when we left her at home
and went to the war,   with a baby at her breast,
a boy, yet by now   he must be counted among grown men.
Lucky lad, his dear father   will stand at last and see him,
and he'll enfold his father   – all as it should be.
My wife wouldn't allow me   any sight of my son;
before I'd had that delight   she had murdered me.
Let me tell you this,   and you should store it at heart:
don't land openly   when you come to your own country;
use stealth since, I tell you,   women must not be trusted.

The word 'nostalgia' is made up of the Greek *algos*, 'painful wanting' and *nostos*, 'return home'. Yet the actual return often turns out a disappointment. Things are not as they were remembered.

THE ENIGMA OF PENELOPE

In societies where the men go off to war, a husband may face two moments of particularly acute anxiety. On the day of departure he asks, 'Will I ever come back?': on the day of return, 'Are things as I left them?' Byron in *Don Juan* take a characteristically wry view:

An honest gentleman at his return
    May not have the good fortune of Ulysses;
Not all lone matrons for their husbands mourn,
    Or show the same dislike to suitors' kisses;
The odds are that he finds a handsome urn
    To his memory – and two or three young misses
Born to some friend, who holds his wife and riches; –
And that *his* Argus bites him by – the breeches.

The Roman statuette of Penelope, which so intrigued James Joyce.

Odysseus has been away twenty years; and at the centre of all that has changed sits Penelope. She is the unknown quantity. Frank Budgen recalled James Joyce's sympathetic awareness of this. On the wall of his flat in Zurich, he had a photograph of an ancient statue of Penelope. He asked Budgen and another friend: 'What is she thinking about?' Budgen suggested she was trying to decide which of her suitors would make the most manageable husband; the other man reckoned she was thinking 'I'll give him just one week more'. 'My own idea,' said Joyce, 'is that she is trying to recollect what Ulysses looks like. You see, he had been away many years, and they had no photographs in those days.'

As Odysseus goes about surreptitiously gaining intelligence, he finds some things just as they were when he departed, others much altered. The landscape is the same, Eumaeus' way of life is constant, except that he has to supply pork for the suitors; the old fountain of Ithacus with its Nymphs is still there, but men like the suitors' servant Melanthius now pass by there. Argos is a reminder of the pursuits Odysseus enjoyed before he left for Troy; but, like Odysseus' own father Laertes, instead of being honoured and cared for in his old age, the faithful hunting dog is cast out in squalor. Eurycleia recognises the old scar, but her cry of joy must be stifled. The past cannot be restored until the present has been purged.

The greatest change that has come about is the disruptive behaviour the suitors have brought to the house of Odysseus. There is nothing intrinsically wrong with their pursuits of wooing, eating, listening to poetry, and making love; but they woo another man's wife, and eat his animals, they force the bard to perform against his will, and they sleep with the maidservants of another's household.

Before Odysseus left, Ithaca was a well-ordered society with a good king. This is one reason why, at the start of the poem, Athena complained to Zeus that her protegé should be allowed to go home:

Why, I wonder, should   any ruler be keen to be kind,
mild and fair-minded?   He might just as well be always
cruel and unscrupulous,   since none of Odysseus' subjects
remember his rule,   which was fair as a father's.

The challenge which faces Odysseus is not only to overcome the suitors and to reclaim his wife, it is also to re-establish a civilised society on Ithaca. This preoccupation lies behind the very first words that he speaks to Penelope for twenty years. She asks the old vagrant who he is and where he comes from. He replies:

My lady, no mortal   in the wide world could condemn you.
Your good repute reaches   high even as heaven,
like a kindly king,   who rules respecting the gods,
and lays down good order   among a powerful people.
The tilth of the earth   bears barley and millet,
orchards and gardens   are heavy with harvest,
sheep bear live lambs,   the sea shoals full with fish,
all thanks to his kindness.   So prosper his people.
So in your house ask   me anything other than
to tell of my family   or of my fatherland,
so you don't fill me fuller   of mourning, as I remember.
I am a man of much   sorrow; and I should not sit
wailing and weeping   in someone else's house.

Before Penelope goes to bed at the end of their long interview, she recalls the beauty and order of the palace of Odysseus when she first came there. The context is particularly poignant, since it comes at the moment when she determines that she must at last leave this house:

This dawn will be a dark one   for me, since it will part me
from Odysseus' household.   I mean to set a contest,
the test of the axe-heads.   He often used to fix them
here in his hall,   twelve in a row like keel-blocks,
and standing well away   would fire an arrow through them.
Now I shall organise   this contest for my suitors:
the one whose hands   most nimbly string the bow,
and shoot the shaft   down through the dozen axe-heads,
him I agree to marry,   deserting my bridal home,
a happy place   and full of good life –
I'll never forget it,   remembered even in my dreaming.

The next day will be the day of the great contest, and Penelope, will, as she says, go to bed with the man who succeeds in the test of Odysseus' bow.

One of a series of terracotta reliefs produced on the island of Melos in the mid-fifth century BC. Presumably the man standing before Penelope is the 'beggar' Odysseus. The seated figure behind her may be Eumaeus.

7 HAPPY THE MAN

You must always have Ithaca in your mind,
Arrival there is your predestination.

Constantine Cavafy

In the world of the *Odyssey* there is a proper sequence to a day of leisure among prosperous people in peacetime, such as at the court of Alcinous on Scherie or of Menelaus at Sparta. The daylight hours are largely spent in exercise and in preparing for the feast, and there may be athletic contests. In the evening baths and fresh clothing make ready for the eating and drinking, which overlap with poetry, music and dance. Finally everyone goes to bed, to love-making and sleep.

The day to which Odysseus awakes in his palace is a distorted version of this underlying pattern, though the suitors do not realise this:

Many beasts had been butchered,   and the suitors were
                                                                        laughing
as they prepared   for a sumptuous supper.
But there could hardly have   been a bitterer banquet
than the one that the man   and the goddess were going to serve
                                                                        them.
They were at fault, after all,   for beginning the business.

Because it is a festival to Apollo the feast is to be even more lavish than usual – Eumaeus has to supply three pigs instead of the customary one.

The competition that supplies the day's sport has as its prize the very person who organises it. The moment when Penelope fetches the bow from the store-room is one of great pathos:

Stretching up to the peg   she lifted off the bow,
still inside the shining   casing of its cover.
Next she sat down   with the case across her knees,
and wept out loud   as she took out her husband's bow.

Penelope just after she has taken down Odysseus' bow from its peg in the storeroom – yet another haunting image from Henry Fuseli.

THE FEAST OF SLAUGHTER

A properly ordered day includes the proper treatment of guests. Wherever you turn in the *Odyssey* there is the theme of hospitality, its proprieties and abuse. Telemachus meets with full and civilised hospitality at Pylos and Sparta; so does Odysseus on Scherie. He also

finds rustic simplicity and the treatment proper to a poor man at Eumaeus' farm. First the rituals of welcome are attended to – the provision of a bath and feast – and only then are questions of identity and business raised. Special emphasis is laid on the guest-gifts, which are seen as an appropriate use of a rich man's wealth – the rule is 'give as you would be given unto'. Telemachus at Sparta and Odysseus on Scherie go away loaded down with gold and silver and fine cloth.

On his wanderings Odysseus encounters all sorts of perversions of the rules of hospitality. The Lotus-eaters forget to ask any questions or to do anything after eating; Circe gives her guests a meal but then turns them into pigs – or takes them to bed if they are immune. Polyphemus is worst of all: he asks questions straight away, and instead of making his guests a meal, he makes one out of them. At first Odysseus had hoped for guest-gifts. Polyphemus remembers this the next evening when he has drunk the wine, and offers Odysseus a special favour:

> Noman shall be munched   last, after all his friends;
> first I'll feast on the rest.   That's to be my guest-gift.

Finally, he throws rocks after his visitor instead of giving him treasure.

Within Odysseus' own palace, because the proprieties of civilised life are disrupted, Telemachus is not able to behave as a proper host. The suitors have not only taken over the hall for their own use; in their confidence and arrogance they do not care about hospitality or considerate behaviour. Very soon after Odysseus first gains entry, Antinous, instead of giving the beggar some food, throws a stool at him. The 'beggar' prays for retribution:

> If there be gods for beggars,   their avengers, may Antinous
> share a deep sleep with death   before any honeymoon.

Antinous has already singled himself out to receive the first arrow. Later in the evening Eurymachus also throws a stool at Odysseus but misses – Eurymachus is the second to die. Next day, before the contest of the bow, Ctesippus throws a cow's hoof at Odysseus, who ducks it. This goads Telemachus to protest:

> . . . I beg of you   stop this spiteful behaviour.
> If you're keen to kill me,   I would rather that fate than
> continue looking on   humiliations in my hall,
> guests getting beaten,   and my maids manhandled.

They are reduced to silence by this new authoritative tone.

When it comes to the contest, none of the suitors can string the bow. As Odysseus strings it, he is likened to a bard stringing his instrument.

> Next he plucked it with his   fingers testing the string,
> and it sang out sweetly   like the call of the swallow.

Like the swallow in spring, the house-builder has returned.

After the contest comes the feast. Odysseus grimly runs the two together:

> Now it's time to set   dinner for these young bloods
> in daylight, and after   to go on to song
> and to music-making   – these properly follow the feast.

The breathtakingly powerful sequence in which the slaughter of the suitors is recounted opens our book. The poetry here achieves a kind of cinematic effect, vivid shots in a tightly edited sequence: Odysseus up on the threshold, Antinous in his blind ignorance below, the suitors on the verge of recognition, the poet's own voice in collusion with the avenger:

> . . . the fools didn't realise the truth –
> that the rope-ends of death   were fastened over every one.
> Subtle Odysseus   said with an angry frown:
> 'Dogs, you were so damned sure   I'd never come home from Troy,
> and so you ransacked   my possessions, and made my maids
> submit in your beds,   and wooed my wife with me still alive.
> You had no dread   for the gods who hold wide heaven,
> nor for any resentment   felt by men in future.
> So now the rope-ends of death   are fastened over you,
> every one.'

The bitter analogy between the feast and the slaughter is sustained. The very first arrow reverses the wine that Antinous was about to drink into a jet of blood from his throat; and it makes him kick over his table loaded with food. There are constant reminders that all this is happening in the great hall, the place of feasting, music and dance. Food and drink are spilled all over the floor and they are smeared and mixed with blood. The suitors try to use the tables as shields against Odysseus' arrows. They are finally reduced to panic, like a herd of stampeding cattle – the animals they have been so greedily consuming.

FUSELI: 'ALL FIRE'

The slaughter of the suitors inspired the artist Henry Fuseli to one of his most dramatic drawings. He was perhaps the prime visual portrayer of the eighteenth-century Romantic cult of Homer. In the 1760s and 1770s in Europe there was a reaction, particularly in Germany, against the artificiality and ornamentation of the baroque era, and a rejection of everything regarded as 'classical' or French, in favour of honesty and sublimity, and the art of the people. The two greatest heroes of the movement were Homer and Shakespeare, as opposed to Virgil and Racine. Fuseli (born Heinrich Füssli in Zürich in 1741) was already illustrating Shakespeare when he was 'discovered' by the British ambassador in Berlin in 1765, and brought to London, where he spent the rest of his long life. He became Keeper of the Royal Academy, was a friend and admirer of William

An engraving by Fuseli captures the moment when Athena helps Odysseus in the slaughter of the suitors.

Blake, and a teacher of, among others, Constable.

Shakespeare, Milton and Homer were his favourite authors. For him they represented the sublime in literature, as Michelangelo and the ancient Greeks did in the visual arts. He helped the poet William Cowper with his translations of the *Odyssey*; Cowper described him as 'All fire, and an enthusiast in the highest degree on the subject of Homer.' His drawings, with their dynamic composition and unusual perspectives, were made into engravings for Cowper's edition, published in 1810. (Nonetheless, it failed to supersede the superb, yet highly artificial translation of Alexander Pope, and when John Keats rejected Pope's Homer, he turned not to Cowper but to the translation made by Shakespeare's contemporary George Chapman.)

As seen on page 15, Fuseli graphically illustrates the scene of slaughter described by Homer: Odysseus and Telemachus and their two helpers occupy the high ground of the threshold of the great hall, whose doors open into the courtyard of the palace. The only other ground-level door out of the hall leads to the women's quarters, and Odysseus has had this locked from the other side by Eurycleia. There is also some kind of opening higher up through which the treacherous servant Melanthius fetches armour for the suitors, until he is captured.

At this point, when almost everyone in the hall has been killed, the blind bard Phemius grasps Odysseus' knees and pleads for his life. Odysseus spares him because only the poet can give him immortal fame. The human desire to have one's name made perpetual finds a wide range of expressions. Heinrich Schliemann hoped, thanks to his excavation at Troy, to be remembered 'as long as there are admirers of Homer in the world, nay as long as this world will be inhabited by men.' James Joyce refused to reveal all the secrets of *Ulysses*, saying: 'I've put in so many enigmas and puzzles that it will keep the professors busy for centuries arguing over what I meant, and that's the only way of ensuring one's immortality.'

Odysseus is not so merciful to all the members of his house. He has the disloyal maidservants – they are twelve out of fifty – drag the bodies of the suitors out into the courtyard and clean up the hall, before they themselves are hung in a row on a line outside. He then orders a great fire to be lit and fumigates the hall with sulphur. Now at last it is time for real music and dance:

> Before all else they bathed   and put on new tunics.
> The women wore their jewellery,   and Phemius the musician
> played his polished lyre,   and so inspired the desire
> in them for sweet singing   and for ceremonious dancing.
> Throughout the great hall   the noise sounded and resounded
> of men's feet in time with   well-dressed women dancing.
> If anyone heard from outside   the house, they would say:
> 'At last one of the suitors   must have married the mistress.
> So she couldn't endure,   and keep her household secure
> for her lawful husband   right through until his return.'
> So they would say, little knowing   what in truth had happened.

In a sense, though, it is a premature wedding celebration for Penelope.

PENELOPE'S PERSPECTIVE

The proper end of the evening at Sparta was briefly told:

> Menelaus went to sleep   deep inside his palace,
> where Helen lay by him, elegant,   a wonder among women.

So too on Scherie:

> Alcinous went to bed   deep inside his palace,
> where his wife the queen   spent the night with him.

Penelope unravelling her tapestry by night provided Joseph Wright of Derby (1734–97) with the kind of shadowy scene he liked to paint. Note the gloomy Argos on the left.

On Ithaca, however, the marriage bedroom has remained locked and unused for twenty years.

Odysseus built his marriage bedroom on the ground floor: the rooms where Penelope has worked and slept throughout the years of his absence are upstairs. Here she wove the great cloth which she then unpicked every night to deceive the suitors, since she had promised to remarry when it was completed. Here she cried herself into dream-filled sleep, night after night, year after year. As the crisis of the contest of the bow approaches, Telemachus asserts his new authority once more:

'Depart to your quarters, take care of your own tasks,
the spindle and the loom; and summon your maidservants
to carry out their work. The bow is men's business,
and mine more than anyone – the master here in this house.'
And she in astonishment went quietly to her quarters,
taking to her heart her son's sensible speech.
Taking her steps upstairs among her handmaidens,
she sighed for Odysseus her husband, until sweet sleep
was slid over her lids by the glinting-eyed goddess Athena.

The wife who has waited so long sleeps throughout the great scene of revenge. When Eurycleia comes cackling to her bedroom with the news, it is all over, and Odysseus is already purifying the hall.

Up till now, it is Odysseus who has done all the testing. Earlier he outwitted Penelope with his inside knowledge of the garments that she made for her husband before he set off for Troy. Now she will out-test the stranger before she will accept him as her true bed-mate. This is her moment of triumph. She tells Eurycleia to take the bed out of the marital bedroom and to make it up for him:

> So she spoke, testing out   her husband; but Odysseus
> said to his wise wife   with a swift pang of anger:
> 'Your words, wife, have wounded   me and hit me hard.
> What man tell me, has   been moving my bed about?'

Only Odysseus, Penelope and one maid know the secret of the bed's construction: how it was built round an olive stock still rooted in the ground. So who, Odysseus asks indignantly, could have moved it? At last Penelope runs across the room and embraces him. As welcome to her as land to shipwrecked sailors when swimming for their lives:

> So welcome to her was   her husband as she beheld him,
> unable to unbind   her creamy arms from his neck.
> Dawn's first fingers   of rose might have risen on them
> still sobbing, but that Athena   decided to detain night,
> and hold dawn's horses   from bringing morning to men.

The Swiss painter Angelica Kauffmann chose the exclusively female moment when Eurycleia goes upstairs to wake Penelope after the slaughter is all over (1772).

All traditional romances lead towards marriage and the establishment of a secure household. The reunion of Odysseus and Penelope in their bed seems to be the perfect happy ending. She is too realistic, however, to pretend that theirs has been a perfect life together – they have, after all, been separated for twenty years:

> The gods have given us misery,
> jealous of the joy   of us two staying together
> all through the fullness of life   and on to the door of old age.

But now, at least, they are together again: the *Odyssey* has reached its long-awaited consummation:

> While they were talking thus   between the two of them,
> Eurynome and the nurse   were spreading the old bed
> with soft sheets and covers   by the light of flaming torches.
> When they had done   with busily making the bed
> the old one went   off to her own bedroom;
> and Eurynome acted   as the bridal attendant,
> and led their steps,   carrying the light for the couple.
> She led them to the bedroom,   then went back, while they
> with a warm welcome   returned to their old bed.

HAPPY EVER AFTER?

Happy endings are always in demand. In the seventeenth and eighteenth centuries, opera took dozens of classical myths – mostly tragic – and concluded them with joyful duets. *Il Ritorno d'Ulisse in Patria* provided Monteverdi's librettist Giacomo Badoara with a golden opportunity in 1641. After a long-delayed recognition, echoing that in the *Odyssey*, Penelope gives in: 'Yes, now I recognise you, yes, now I believe you. . .' and they end up singing in unison:

> Now the day of pleasure, the day of delight has come.
> Yes, yes, my life, yes, yes, my heart, yes, yes.
> (*Si, si vita! si si core, si si!*)

Throughout the centuries, the end of Odysseus' travels has been used by creative artists as a symbol of affirmation, yet few have been able to achieve the unmixed joy of Badoaro's libretto. Poets have found in it a kind of analogy or counter-analogy with their own lot. The Roman poet Ovid, for example, banished by the emperor Augustus to the shores of the Black Sea and longing for Rome, turned away from the villainous Odysseus of his earlier poetry and identified himself again and again with the husband who returned. Ovid died in exile however. Conversely, the French poet Joachim du Bellay, who spent some years as a diplomat among the splendours of Rome, expressed in his sonnets *Les Regrets*, published in 1558, a longing for his home village in Anjou. The most famous begins: '*Heureux qui, comme Ulysse, a fait un beau voyage . . .*':

> Happy the man who's journeyed much, like Ulysses,
> Or like the traveller who won the Golden Fleece,

Monteverdi's Il Ritorno d'Ulisse in Patria *at Glyndebourne in 1979. Penelope (played by Frederika von Stade) stands isolated, with Eurycleia and the disguised Odysseus on one side, Eumaeus in rustic garb and Telemachus on the other.*

And has returned at last, experienced and wise,
To end his days among his family in peace.
When will I see again, oh when, the woodsmoke rise
Above my village chimneys, under my own skies
See once again my humble, narrow plot, which is
A whole wide realm to me, and so much more besides?
I hold more dear my house, my poor ancestral home
Than all the splendid palaces of haughty Rome:
Dearer far than cold marble the slate's subtle blue;
More than Latin Tiber this Gallic Loire of mine,
More my little Liré than the proud Palatine
And more than Rome's salt air the sweetness of Anjou.

Yet in a later sonnet, when his return is imminent, Odysseus' happiness loses some of its glow even for du Bellay:

Like Ulysses again, I thought how sweet
To see above my roof the woodsmoke rise . . .
But after a weary absence of years
I find even at home a thousand cares . . .

153

ITHACA IN EXILE

The earlier of du Bellay's poems is closer to the spirit of the *Odyssey* than Ovid is because, like Odysseus, the poet has chosen to return to a familiar but insignificant home, even though this means that he must sacrifice the exciting events of the great metropolis. It is ironic that Ithaca has become somewhere on the map solely because Odysseus opted for its obscurity. The great story of his return to his lowly homeland has turned what would otherwise have been an obscure little island into one of the world's more significant names.

Today Ithaca is still off the beaten track and remarkably unspoilt. It is easy for visiting foreigners to hope that the island will continue free of package holidays. But the wife of the schoolteacher at Stavros told us sadly that many of the children who go to Athens to finish their education do not return to sleepy Ithaca. For them, the lure of the capital is too great. Others have left for harsher reasons. The terrible earthquake of 1953 destroyed 90 per cent of Vathý's buildings and took many lives. The population of the island – then around 8000 – was halved in the resulting exodus. Many are now living in America and Australia.

This is a phenomenon repeated all over Greece: from the heart of the Peloponnese and from its extremities, from Euboea and Corinth, Corfu, Chios and the other islands, hundreds of thousands of Greeks have been scattered in a shifting diaspora all round the world. It is alleged that, after Athens, the two largest Greek communities in the world are to be found in Melbourne and Chicago.

The *Odyssey* has always spoken to exiles, above all those from Greece. For Constantine Cavafy, born in Alexandria in Egypt in 1863, Ithaca herself had nothing to offer; her value lay in the journey there:

> Setting out on the voyage to Ithaca
> You must pray that the way be long,
> full of adventures and experiences. . .
>
> You must pray that the way be long;
> Many be the summer mornings
> When with what pleasure, with what delight
> You enter harbours never seen before. . .
>
> You must always have Ithaca in your mind,
> Arrival there is your predestination.
> But do not hurry the journey at all.
> Better that it should last many years;
> Be quite old when you anchor at the island,
> Rich with all you have gained on the way,
> Not expecting Ithaca to give you riches.
> Ithaca has given you your lovely journey.
> Without Ithaca you would not have set out.
> Ithaca has no more to give you now.

*George Seferis, a poet worthy
of the language of Homer.*

Symbol of Joyce *by
Constantin Brancusi (1929) –
though the symbol rather lacks
Joyce's rich complexity.*

Poor though you find it, Ithaca has not cheated you.
Wise as you have become, with all your experience,
You will have understood the meaning of an Ithaca.

Cavafy turns Odysseus into Everyman. By putting 'you', his reader, into the role of the voyager, he opens up the experience – for Greeks and non-Greeks alike – and achieves a remarkable accessibility.

George Seferis is a more difficult poet, an appropriate translator of T. S. Eliot into modern Greek. He is, however, one of the greatest of all the poets of our century, deservedly awarded the Nobel Prize for literature in 1963. Odysseus and the *Odyssey* are profoundly and pervasively interwoven in his work, from his 24-poem series *Mythistorema* (1935) to his last poems, written under the tyranny of the Junta in Athens in 1971. Seferis was born in Smyrna in 1900, educated in Paris, and served as a diplomat for most of his life in various countries of the Middle East before becoming ambassador in London from 1957–62. All Greeks in Smyrna (which they had to abandon in 1922 when they were driven out by the Turks amid terrible bloodshed) were taught that Homer was a native of the city and that they were his descendants. School parties were taken to the banks of the river Meles which, according to an ancient legend, was Homer's father.

At Christmas 1931, in London, remembering du Bellay and his own lost homeland, Seferis wrote *Reflections on a foreign line of verse*. He begins:

Happy the man who has completed the voyage of Odysseus. . .

Yet after this he conjures up a far more haunting Odysseus:

And again and again the shade of Odysseus appears before me,
	his eyes red from the waves' salt,
from his ripe longing to see once more the smoke ascending from
	his warm hearth and the dog grown old waiting by the door.
A large man, whispering through his whitened beard words in
	our language spoken as it was three thousand years ago. . .

By the end of the poem it is clear that Seferis sees the whole of his life as a desolate Odyssey, with – unlike du Bellay – no real prospect of ever completing the voyage:

He tells me of the harsh pain you feel when the ship's sails swell
	with memory and your soul becomes a rudder;
of being alone, dark in the night, and helpless as chaff on the
	threshing floor;
of the bitterness of seeing your companions one by one pulled
	down into the elements and scattered;
and of how strangely you gain strength conversing with the dead
	when the living who remain are no longer enough.
He speaks . . . I still see his hands that knew how to judge the
	carving of the mermaid at the prow
presenting me the waveless blue sea in the heart of winter.

A more amusingly Joycean portrait by Guy Davenport (1964) – with Molly's bloomers in hand?

MOLLY'S MELONS

James Joyce was an exile, too. The last words printed on the last page of *Ulysses* are

'Trieste–Zurich–Paris'
1914–1921

The homecomings of this book are characteristically multiple, though underlying their complexities is the fundamental polarity of man and woman.

The penultimate section of the book, which was originally labelled *Ithaca*, takes the form of a question and answer catechism. It covers Bloom's return to 7 Eccles Street in the small hours of the morning (17 June 1904). Immediately he is faced with a problem, because he has left his key in another pair of trousers. He has to climb over the railings and get in through the scullery door – not unlike Odysseus' furtive return as a beggar. As with Odysseus, there have been other men in his house: on the piano is 'Love's Old Sweet Song' which Molly has been practising with her current suitor, Blazes Boylan.

Bloom is with Stephen Dedalus, a young intellectual, and the hero of Joyce's earlier, semi-autobiographical work *Portrait of the Artist as a Young Man*. For this night Bloom has looked after Stephen, as if he were his son, some compensation for the loss of his own Rudy, who would have been his future. The substitute Telemachus departs after a cup of Epp's Soluble Cocoa, declining the offer of a bed for the night. Stephen is soon to set off on his travels. His itinerary has been a favourite subject of dispute among Joyceans. One suggestion is that he goes out of 7 Eccles Street to leave Dublin and to create *Ulysses* – Bloom's Phemius?

Bloom, left alone, imagines doing a bunk himself and embarking on great wanderings:

> What tributes his?
> Honour and gifts of strangers, the friends of Everyman.
> A nymph immortal, beauty, the bride of Noman.
> . . .
> Would the departed never nowhere nohow reappear?
> Ever would he wander, selfcompelled, to the extreme limit of his cometary orbit, beyond the fixed stars and variable suns and telescopic planets, astronomical waifs and strays, to the extreme boundary of space, passing from land to land, among peoples amid events.

He must somehow be recalled, however, and somehow:

> . . . return an estranged avenger, a wreaker of justice on malefactors, a dark crusader, a sleeper awakened, with financial resources (by supposition) surpassing those of Rothschild or the silver king.

This pan-galactic Odysseus comes characteristically back down to earth. He prefers to be reconciled with his lot rather than to play the hero, and he soon thinks of reasons for staying put:

The lateness of the hour, rendering procrastinatory: the obscurity of the night, rendering invisible: the uncertainty of thoroughfares, rendering perilous: the necessity for repose, obviating movement: the proximity of an occupied bed, obviating research: the anticipation of warmth (human). . .

So Leopold Bloom settles for the 'occupied bed'.

Far from being an immutable olive-rooted bed, unused for twenty years, this bed has come 'all the way from Gibraltar' where Molly's father bought it off 'old Cohen'. Victor Bérard in his reconstruction of Odysseus' voyages had located Calypso on an island off Gibraltar, so Molly's birthplace becomes part of Joyce's fusion of Penelope and Calypso. The bed has followed the couple around a succession of abodes, and has welcomed a succession of Molly's lovers. Now Bloom climbs in:

How?

With circumspection, as invariably when entering an abode (his own or not his own): with solicitude, the snakespiral springs of the mattress being old, the brass quoits and pendant viper radii loose and tremulous under stress and strain: prudently, as entering a lair or ambush of lust or adders: lightly the less to disturb: reverently, the bed of conception and of birth, of consummation of marriage and of breach of marriage, of sleep and of death.

What did his limbs, when gradually extended, encounter? New clean bedlinen, additional odours, the presence of a human form, female, hers, the imprint of a human form, male, not his, some crumbs, some flakes of potted meat, recooked, which he removed.

Boylan has been enjoying Plumtree's Potted Meat in this 'abode of bliss'. Yet Bloom prefers equanimity to jealousy, and rejects Odyssean vengeance. It is characteristic of him to prefer compromise; this, in a sense, is his triumph.

What retribution, if any?
Assassination, never, as two wrongs did not make one right.
Dual by combat, no. Divorce, not now. . .

He justifies these sentiments to himself by reflecting on:

the futility of triumph or protest or vindication: the inanity of extolled virtue: the lethargy of nescient matter: the apathy of the stars.

Equanimity is Bloom's version of stringing and shooting the bow – a kind of victory over the vigorous insensitivity of the likes of Boylan.

So he kisses the 'yellow smellow melons' of Molly's rump, half-answers her sleepy questions, and curling up, head to tail, drifts off to sleep. 'He rests. He has travelled.' Yet the chapter does not end there but with a question:

Where?

THE OTHER HALF OF THE BED

Ulysses does not end with the man but with the woman, with a flow
of words that Joyce entitled *Penelope*. The *Odyssey*, despite Samuel
Butler's theories about its authorship, is a male poem with a pre-
dominantly male perspective. Suzanne Vega asks what it was like for
Calypso after Odysseus had gone. Hers is a proud but not a happy
song. Penelope does not take part at all in the closing scenes of the
Odyssey; and Joyce's ending may be interpreted as in some ways
more sympathetic to the female perspective.

Penelope consists of the thoughts that go through Molly's dozing
mind – 25,000 words without one single mark of punctuation other
than the initial asterisk and the final full stop. It begins with a
thought about her husband:

> *Yes because he never did a thing like that before as ask to get his
> breakfast in bed. . .

*The finale of Monteverdi's
opera* Il Ritorno d'Ulisse in
Patria. *'Si si vita! Si, si core,
si si!'*

But she muses, as her thoughts progress, on Boylan and many other lovers. Of all of Joyce's calculated departures from the *Odyssey*, the greatest is the repeated infidelity of his Penelope. Molly is not inclined to abandon Bloom, but she has no intention of becoming faithful to him either:

> Ill just give him one more chance Ill get up early in the morning Im sick of Cohens old bed in any case I might go over to the markets to see all the vegetables and cabbages and tomatoes and carrots and all kinds of splendid fruits all coming in lovely and fresh who knows whod be the 1st man Id meet. . .

But, as we reach the last page of this 'epic', Molly's mind returns to the first time that she and Bloom made love out on Howth Head:

> it was leapyear like now yes 16 years ago my God after that long kiss I near lost my breath yes he said I was a flower of the mountain yes so we are flowers all a womans body yes that was one true thing he said in his life and the sun shines for you today yes that was why I liked him because I saw he understood or felt what a woman is and I knew I could always get round him and I gave him all the pleasure I could leading him on till he asked me to say yes and I wouldnt answer first only looked out over the sea and the sky I was thinking of so many things he didnt know of. . .

This Penelope is not only the equal of her husband's subtlety – she knows that she can get round him at any time. Molly also arrives at a kind of compromise: even in the last lines she is still merging the 'he' of Bloom with other past lovers. Yet her husband is her last thought:

> . . . and Gibraltar as a girl where I was a Flower of the mountain yes when I put the rose in my hair like the Andalusian girls used or shall I wear a red yes and how he kissed me under the Moorish wall and I thought well as well him as another and then I asked him with my eyes to ask again yes and then he asked me would I yes to say yes my mountain flower and first I put my arms around him yes and drew him down to me so he could feel my breasts all perfume yes and his heart was going like mad and yes I said yes I will Yes.

This is hardly the simple affirmation of Monteverdi: *Si si vita! Si si, core, si si!* Molly's affections are as all-embracing and as wide-ranging as her bed.

8 TO PAUSE, TO MAKE AN END?

We all are homeless sometimes, homesick sometimes,
As we all at times are godless or godfearing –
And what does that imply?

Louis MacNeice, Day of Returning

Odysseus *by Georges Braque,*
done in black and white chalk
in about 1931.

They with a warm welcome   returned to their old bed.

And yet there is a shadow cast over this almost happy-ever-after ending. As though that would be too good to be true, Homer disturbs the future with yet further ordeals for Odysseus. When he visited the Underworld, the ghost of Teiresias, the blind soothsayer, told him what he would have to do once he was home:

Afterwards set off   taking your balanced oarblade,
till you come to a country   where the sea means nothing to
them;
where they eat their meat   without seasoning of salt–
men who haven't even heard   of ships with their painted sides
or balanced oarblades,   which work as wings for ships.
I'll tell you a token,   an unmistakable symbol:
when on your journey   you meet a man who assumes
that the oar on your shoulder's   a shovel carved for winnowing
corn, then plant your blade   solidly in the soil,
and make sacrifices   to powerful Poseidon,
a black bull, a boar   that mounts sows, and a ram.
Then make your way homeward,   and offer sacrifices
to all the immortals,   who hold heaven, in due order.
And death, O so softly,   will find you off the sea,
and will finish you   weakened by an easy old age.
About you your people shall   thrive. All this is true.

This is a mysterious prophecy, which seems to be in part some kind of final propitiation of Poseidon. There is a problem, three lines from the end, in the Greek: some scholars say that it means that Odysseus will meet his death 'far from the sea'; but if 'homeward', two lines earlier, means home to Ithaca, then it must mean 'out of the sea'. There was an ancient epic (now lost), the *Telegony*, which told how Odysseus had a son by Circe, Telegonus, and how he killed Odysseus in battle without realising that he was his father. And yet that hardly fits with the easy old age which Teiresias prophesies. The problem remains unsolved.

In other later and more scurrilous versions, Odysseus was alleged to have fathered eighteen children by six different females in one place or another. Even Penelope was said to have slept with one, several or all of the suitors; and another story made her mother of the wild god Pan, with Hermes as his father. In the *Odyssey*, however, there is no hint that they will not remain faithful ever after.

PENELOPE'S FUTURE

Yet all is not well. When Odysseus and Penelope are finally in each other's arms, and Athena has held up the dawn, a strangely awkward conversation takes place between them:

> Then subtle Odysseus   said these words to his wife:
> 'Wife, we haven't yet come   to the limits of our trials;
> there's still a labour left,   immeasurably immense
> and difficult to do,   which I must endure to the end.
> Thus Teiresias'   spirit prophesied that day
> I descended to Hades   to learn about our return.
> But let's stir ourselves   and lie at long last in our bed,
> taking due delight   in sleeping sweetly together.'
> Penelope then in turn   prudently responded:
> 'The time for bed shall be   whenever your heart wants it,
> seeing that the gods   have brought you back home
> to your firm-founded house   and the fields of your fathers.
> But since you thought of this   and a god put it in your spirit,
> tell me of this trial.   I'm bound to learn of it later,
> so it would be none the worse   to know about it now.'
> Then subtle Odysseus   said these words in response:
> 'Why on earth urge me   so strongly to tell you?
> In that case, I'll say   without concealment –
> you won't be overjoyed, though,   I feel no delight myself,
> since he told me I must visit   all sorts of cities
> holding in my hands   my balanced oarblade
> till I come to a country' . . .

Odysseus then gives Teiresias' prophecy word for word. Penelope's resonse is:

> If the gods determine   a better old age to be,
> then there's still hope   there'll be release from ills.

These are the very last words that Penelope speaks in the *Odyssey*. They are words of reassurance and optimism, despite the language that Odysseus himself has used of the trials which lie ahead. Who can say which of the two is misjudging the future?

The last words that are addressed to Penelope in the *Odyssey* have not been much noticed. On the following morning Odysseus is setting out to visit his estates and to see his old father. He foresees that there will be trouble:

> Wise though you may be, wife,   listen to what I tell you:

once the sun rises there's bound to be some rumours
about the fate of the suitors whom I slaughtered in my hall,
so go upstairs and stay there among your maidservants.
Don't look at anyone, and don't ask any questions.

It is true that in the final book of the poem Penelope is paid a tribute by the ghost of Agamemnon who contrasts her with Clytemnestra. But her own husband's final tribute is to send her peremptorily off to her housework and to isolation. This is a far cry from the independence and power ascribed to queen Arete of the Phaeacians, from Calypso or, indeed, from Molly Bloom. So, does the *Odyssey* end happily for Penelope? Someone should write her story. Does the *Odyssey* end happily even for Odysseus?

DEATH AT ZERO-POINT

The Odysseus who abandons Penelope and goes on searching and wandering has been a persistent shadow in European literature. Nikos Kazantzakis' *The Odyssey. A Modern Sequel* (at 33,333 lines, over twice as long as Homer, and even longer than James Joyce's *Ulysses*) picks up the story after the slaughter of the suitors:

> And when in his white courtyards Odysseus had cut down
> The insolent youths, he hung on high his sated bow . . .

Penelope, *an oil painting by David Ligare (1984). Note the post-modernist Grecian chair.*

An illustration by the Greek artist Ghika to accompany Kazantzakis' The Odyssey. A Modern Sequel (1938): Odysseus deserts the sleeping Penelope after only one night at home.

But Penelope cannot accept this butcher, nor can he accept her ('he saw his wife still tangled in their naked forms'). He needs more exploits: 'and his wild tiger heart in darkness licked its lips'. The Odysseus of Kazantzakis slips from Penelope's bed the next morning, loots his own palace, and sets sail, telling his men 'look no longer at Ithaca: we shall never see it again'. He roams continents, explores jungles, founds cities, becomes a holy man, all in quest of the liberation of the self. In the end he dies peacefully on an iceberg in Antarctica, 'Zero-point of the earth' as W. B. Stanford puts it.

The Italian poet Guido Pascoli, in his poem *Last Voyage* (1904), creates a much more passive and melancholy Odysseus. After nine monotonous years on Ithaca, he hears the song of the swallow and departs with his companions, who sing a traditional children's swallow-song to the accompaniment of Phemius' lyre. He plans to revisit the scenes of his great adventures, but the voyage brings no glory and no insight. When Odysseus asks the Sirens for knowledge, above all an answer to the questions 'Who am I, who shall I be?', they do not reply; and his only answer is the sight of the skeletons on their shore. Odysseus is finally washed up on Calypso's luxuriant island, where she hides his dead body in the cloud of her hair.

Gabriele d'Annunzio is at the opposite pole from this poignant acquiescence. The Odysseus of his *The Unaccompanied Hero* is a ruthless entrepreneur, like the one in Sophocles' *Philoctetes*, determined on success. D'Annunzio's attitude of 'who dares wins' proved to be a major intellectual influence on the development of Italian fascism.

NEWS OF ULYSSES

Behind these twentieth-century versions of the restless wanderer lie two great poems. Tennyson's *Ulysses* was written in 1833, soon after the death of his closest friend Arthur Hallam. Tennyson believed that he must press on with life, despite this crushing bereavement. He himself said that there was more of himself in *Ulysses* than in the more directly commemorative *In Memoriam*: 'It gives the feeling,' he said, 'about the need of going forward and braving the struggle of life.' W. H. Auden took issue with the poet's own interpretation: 'What is *Ulysses* but a covert refusal to be a responsible and useful person, a glorification of the heroic dandy?' There is some irony, in view of Auden's own restless history, in the aspersions he casts on that respectable Victorian poet. But this nicely illustrates the capacity of the poem – and indeed of the figure of Odysseus – to include a multiplicity of meanings:

> It little profits that an idle king,
> By this still hearth, among these barren crags,
> Match'd with an aged wife, I meet and dole
> Unequal laws unto a savage race,
> That hoard, and sleep, and feed, and know not me.
> I cannot rest from travel: I will drink
> Life to the lees . . .'

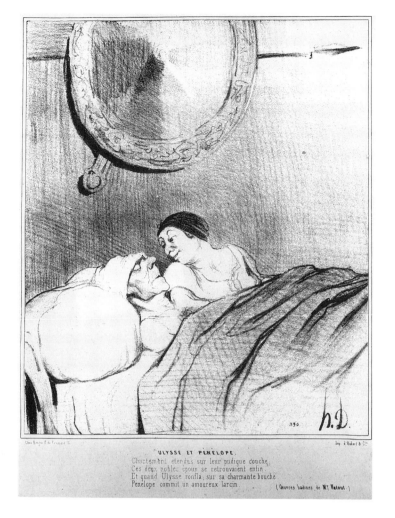

The memory of his past exploits only serves to sharpen his appetite:

> I am a part of all that I have met;
> Yet all experience is an arch wherethro'
> Gleams that untravell'd world, whose margin fades
> For ever and for ever when I move.
> How dull it is to pause, to make an end,
> To rust unburnish'd, not to shine in use!
> As tho' to breathe were life. Life piled on life
> Were all too little, and of one to me
> Little remains: but every hour is saved
> From that eternal silence, something more,
> A bringer of new things; and vile it were
> For some three suns to store and hoard myself,
> And this gray spirit yearning in desire
> To follow Knowledge like a sinking star,
> Beyond the utmost bound of human thought.

So he leaves Ithaca to his conscientious and high-minded son Telemachus. He himself must go on; and he calls on his old crew:

> – you and I are old;
> Old age hath yet his honour and his toil;
> Death closes all: but something ere the end,
> Some work of noble note, may yet be done,
> Not unbecoming men that strove with gods.
> The light begins to twinkle from the rocks:
> The long day wanes: the slow moon climbs: the deep
> Moans round with many voices. Come, my friends,
> 'Tis not too late to seek a newer world.
> Push off, and sitting well in order smite
> The sounding furrows; for my purpose holds
> To sail beyond the sunset, and the baths
> Of all the western stars, until I die.
> It may be that the gulf will wash us down:
> It may be we shall touch the Happy Isles,
> And see the great Achilles, whom we knew.
> Tho' much is taken, much abides; and tho'
> We are not now that strength which in old days
> Moved earth and heaven; that which we are, we are;
> One equal temper of heroic hearts,
> Made weak by time and fate, but strong in will
> To strive, to seek, to find, and not to yield.

Tennyson was soaked in Homer, yet the greater influence here is Dante's *Inferno*. Ulysses is everlastingly damned in the part of Hell reserved for 'fraudulent counsellors', and Dante's guide, Virgil, explains to him that he is there because he was responsible for the Trojan horse and various other deceits. Virgil interrogates the flaming form; and a voice from within it tells of Ulysses' voyage after he left Circe:

> No tenderness for my son, nor piety
> To my old father, nor the wedded love
> That should have comforted Penelope
>
> Could conquer in me the restless itch to rove
> And rummage through the world exploring it,
> All human worth and wickedness to prove.

With a single ship he sailed out through Gibraltar and down the coast of Africa (in the days before Columbus, Dante has him sail south, not west). Eventually he and his companions are wrecked and drowned. His spirit is epitomised by the words with which he encourages his weary men:

> Think of your breed; for brutish ignorance
> Your metal was not made; you were made men,
> To follow after knowledge and excellence.

A fourteenth-century Venetian manuscript of Dante's Inferno, *showing the meeting of Dante and Virgil with the flaming spirit of Ulysses.*

Ulysses' crime as a false counsellor was ultimately, then, to encourage his fellow men in the unlimited search for knowledge.

Dante knew little about ancient Greece, and the text of Homer – in Greek or any other language – was simply not available in his day. The deceitful Ulysses is the standard figure, derived from Roman literature, which was current throughout the Middle Ages. Only in Dante's version, however, does he fail to return home after leaving Circe. Nobody knows whether Dante was following a variant tradition; his immense contribution has been the ever-questing Odysseus, searching inexhaustibly after knowledge and excellence. It was this characteristic humanist drive that was soon to bring an end to the Middle Ages and to inspire the Renaissance.

If the story of Odysseus is regarded as fixed in ancient Greece, then Dante, in his ignorance, has departed from it. However, we are in agreement with the attitude of John Keats who saw the story, not as dead and static, but as perennially alive and growing. Keats' contemporary Leigh Hunt reported in 1819:

> He observed that whenever so great a poet [such as Dante] told us anything in addition or continuation of an ancient story, he had a right to be regarded as a classical authority. For instance, said he, when he tells us of that characteristic death of Ulysses in one of the books of his *Inferno*, we ought to receive the information as authentic, and be glad that we have more news of Ulysses than we looked for.

Keats saw a cumulative wholeness within the diversity of the Ulysses theme.

Looking at the stories of Odysseus as a whole, there seems to be an irreconcilable contradiction between the man who stays on Ithaca and the man who cannot cease from exploration. One longs for security and stability: the bed is the goal of his ordeal, home is his fulfilment. The other cannot rest from adventure and enterprise: he is compelled to go on in the quest for knowledge, even though this means abandoning the safety and fidelity of his wife and of his household.

Two separate Odysseuses? We believe that most women and most men have both within them. One may predominate at any time; and we have always to be choosing between one or the other. But they are both there, conflicting and yet somehow fused within each of us. The whole Odysseus – from Homer to Seferis, from Dante to James Joyce – encompasses both the desire for security and the desire for adventure. This is why our own Odyssey through Troy and Maleia and Ithaca does not in the end arrive. Nor does it in the end depart. It remains an Odyssey round Odysseus.

William Blake's painting
The Circle of the Life of
Man *(1821). Several of the*
figures seem to be inspired by
the Odyssey: *an Athena*
figure stands by the kneeling
'Odysseus'; on the right are a
Penelope and a Nausicaa, and
above them the Nymphs in the
mouth of their cave, carrying
baskets of their weaving.

References to Homer

page	reference	page	reference	page	reference
13	*Od* 22.35–6	61	*Il* 7.84–91	127	*Od* 13.287–95
	21.404–23	63	9.308–13		13.344–58
14	22.1–36		19.216–20,		13.383–6
15	1.1–5		225–32	128	14.1–8
23	11.367–8	64	2.198–205	129	16.187–9
26	22.330–56		2.257–75		17.197–211
28	13.78–80, 88–92	81	8.97	129–30	17.291–304
	13.93–7	82	11.5–9	130	17.326–7
29	11.367–9, 373–6		9.412–15		17.336–41
38	17.382–6		*Od* 24.76–84		19.232–5
39	9.2–11	96–7	8.492–520	131–2	20.5–30
	8.479–81	100	*Il* 3.216–24	132	13.363–73
	11.333–4	102	*Od* 8.521–31	135	13.407–10
40	5.63–73	103	8.572–8	136	9.21–6
41–2	5.215–24		9.19–21	139	14.8–12
42	23.295–6		9.79–81		14.49–51
	23.190–202	106	9.82–4	140	16.190–91
44	5.241–68	107	20.18–21		19.208–12
46	9.528–35		9.172–6	141	11.441–56
	5.368–70	108	9.213–5	142	5.8–12
	5.388–99		9.228–30	143	19.107–20
46–7	23.232–40		9.281–2		19.571–81
47	5.453–7, 462–3		9.299–305	144	20.390–94
	5.488–91	108–10	9.361–76		21.53–6
	5.475–82	110	9.403–14	146	9.369–70
48	6.119–62		9.420–23		17.475–6
49	6.180–85	111	9.456–7		20.314–9
	8.248–9		9.475–9		21.410–11
	6.262–7		9.502–5	147	21.428–30
	6.4–10		9.528–35		22.32–41
50	7.117–28	112	9.19–20	149	23.142–52
54	6.204–5		13.1–2		4.304–5
55	9.27	113	11.14–6, 19		7.346–7
57	8.72–7	116	12.184–91	150	21.350–58
	Il 1.1–2		12.437–41	151	23.181–4
58	1.1–5	116–7	17.233–8		23.239–45
	6.447–65	123	8.555–63	152	23.210–2
59	21.373–6		12.286		23.288–96
	22.56–71	124	7.318–20	160	23.296
	22.147–56		8.444–5		11.121–37
60	22.410–11		13.29–30	161	23.247–68
	22.440–46	125	13.70–92		23.286–7
	22.508–13	126	13.93–124	161–2	23.361–5
	24.795–804				

Recommended reading

THE BEST INTRODUCTORY WORKS
Translations of the *Odyssey* by Walter Shewring (Oxford 1980); Richmond Lattimore
(New York 1965)
Peter V. Jones, *Companion* to Lattimore's translation (Bristol 1988)
Jasper Griffin, *The Odyssey* (Landmarks in World Literature, Cambridge 1987)
Richard Ellman, *James Joyce* (Oxford 1959)
W. B. Stanford, *The Ulysses Theme* (2nd ed. Oxford 1968) – an indispensable study
Oswyn Murray, *Early Greece* (London 1980) and Anthony Snodgrass, *Archaic Greece* (London 1980)
provide historical perspectives

COMMENTARIES ON THE TEXT IN GREEK
There is a brief but good commentary by W. B. Stanford (London 2nd ed. 1959),
and a fuller one by various authors:
Books I–IV by Stephanie West and Books V–VIII by J. B. Hainsworth (Oxford 1988)
Books IX–XII by Alfred Heubeck and Books XIII–XVI by Arie Hoekstra (Oxford 1989)

INTERPRETATIONS
Norman Austin, *Archery at the Dark of the Moon* (California 1975)
Howard Clarke, *The Art of the Odyssey* (Englewood Cliff 1967, repr. Bristol 1989)
George Dimock, *The Unity of the Odyssey* (Amhurst 1989)
Bernard Fenik, *Studies in the Odyssey* (Wiesbaden 1974)
Chris Emlyn-Jones, 'The Reunion of Penelope and Odysseus' (in *Greece and Rome* 31 (1984) 1ff.)
R. B. Rutherford, 'At home and abroad: aspects of the structure of the Odyssey'
(in *Proceedings of the Cambridge Philological Society* N.S 31 (1985) 133ff.)
R. B. Rutherford, 'The Philosophy of the Odyssey' (in *Journal of Hellenic Studies* 106 (1986) 145ff.)
Agathe Thornton, *People and Themes in Homer's Odyssey* (London 1970)
Pierre Vidal-Nacquet, 'Land and Sacrifice in the Odyssey, a study in religious and mythical
meanings' in *The Black Hunter* translated by A. Szegedy-Maszak (Baltimore 1986)

ODYSSEUS/ULYSSES IN LATER ART AND LITERATURE
Harry Blamires, *The Bloomsday Book* (London 1985)
Howard Clarke, *Homer's Readers* (East Brunswick N.J 1981)
David Constantine, *Early Greek Travellers and the Hellenic Ideal* (Cambridge 1984)
Stuart Gilbert, *James Joyce's Ulysses* (London 1960)
Ruth Padel, 'Homer's Reader: A Reading of George Seferis'
(in *Proceedings of the Cambridge Philological Society* N.S 31 (1985) 74ff.)
M. M. Scherer, *The Legend of Troy in Art and Literature* (London 1973)
W. B. Stanford and J. V. Luce, *The Quest for Ulysses* (London 1974)

ITHACA AND TROY

J. M. Cook, *The Troad* (Oxford 1973)

L. Foxall and J. Davis (eds.), *The Trojan War: its Historicity and Context* (Bristol 1984)

Manfred Korfmann 'Troy: topography and navigation' and 'Beşık Tepe: New Evidence. . .'
  (in *Troy and the Trojan War*, ed. M. J. Mellink, Bryn Mawr PA 1986)

Joachim Latacz, 'News from Troy' (in *Berytus* 34, 1986, 97ff.)

J. B. Wace and F. H. Stubbings (eds.), *A Companion to Homer* (London 1952)

Michael Wood, *In Search of the Trojan War* (London 1985)

HISTORICAL BACKGROUND TO HOMER

John Boardman, *The Greeks Overseas* (London 3rd ed. 1980)

J. M. Cook, *The Greeks in Ionia and the East* (London 1962)

M. I. Finley, *Early Greece: the Bronze and Archaic Ages* (London 2nd ed. 1981)

L. H. Jeffery, *Archaic Greece* (London 1976)

The principal Homeric characters and places mentioned

Achaeans	One of Homer's names for the Greeks (he does not call them Greeks or Hellenes).
Achilles	Greatest of the Greek warriors at Troy, he is killed there not long before the sack.
Aeolus	A god who controls the winds.
Agamemnon	Lord of Mycene. He organises the Greeks against Troy on behalf of his brother Menelaus. He is killed by his wife Clytemnestra on his return home.
Ajax	Greatest of the Greek warriors after Achilles. When defeated by Odysseus for the arms of Achilles he kills himself.
Alcinous	King of the Phaeacians who live on Scherie.
Andromache	Wife of Hector of Troy.
Antinous	The ringleader and most unpleasant of the suitors of Penelope.
Apollo	The Olympian god who most favours the Trojans.
Argives	One of Homer's names for the Greeks.
Argos	Odysseus' favourite hunting-dog, left behind on Ithaca.
Athena	Olympian goddess, daughter of Zeus, who takes a special interest in Odysseus.
Calypso	A goddess or nymph who lives by herself on a remote island where she keeps Odysseus for seven years.
Charybdis	A voracious whirlpool, opposite Scylla.
Circe	A goddess or nymph who turns her visitors into animals – or, as with Odysseus, seduces them.

Cyclopes	A race of savage one-eyed giants. The one encountered by Odysseus is Polyphemus.
Demodocus	The blind court poet and musician of the Phaeacians.
Eumaeus	Loyal farmer in charge of Odysseus' pigs.
Eurycleia	Odysseus' old nurse.
Eurymachus	A particularly dastardly suitor.
Hector	The greatest Trojan prince, son of Priam. As told in the *Iliad* he is killed by Achilles.
Hecuba	Queen of Troy, wife of Priam.
Helen	Wife of Menelaus of Sparta, her seduction by Paris led to the Trojan War. Afterwards she returned home with Menelaus.
Hellespont	The mouth of the Dardanelles near Troy.
Hephaestus	Olympian god with special associations with fire and metallurgy.
Hera	Wife of Zeus, powerful goddess.
Ilios, Ilium	Greek names for Troy.
Ithaca	Island off the west of Greece, home of Odysseus.
Laertes	Father of Odysseus. In his son's absence he lives in poverty on a remote farm.
Maleia	The cape at the southeast tip of mainland Greece.
Melanthius	Servant of the suitors who supplies them with meat – particularly treacherous.
Melantho	Sister of Melanthius, ringleader of the unfaithful maidservants of Odysseus' household.
Menelaus	Lord of Sparta. The Trojan War was undertaken to restore his honour after the abduction of his wife Helen.
Nausicaa	Princess on Scherie, daughter of Alcinous.
Nestor	The wise old man of the Greeks at Troy, lord of Pylos.
Neritos	The main mountain on Ithaca.
Paris	Prince of Troy, seducer of Helen.
Peleus	Father of Achilles by his marriage to the sea-goddess Thetis.
Penelope	Wife of Odysseus, besieged by suitors on Ithaca.
Phemius	Poet and musician on Ithaca.
Philoetius	Loyal keeper of Odysseus' cattle.
Phorcys	Old god of the sea.
Polyphemus	Particularly savage Cyclops, son of Poseidon.
Poseidon	Olympian god, second only to Zeus, with special power over the sea.
Priam	Old king of Troy, killed at the sack.
Scamander	Main river of Troy.
Scylla	A voracious female monster, opposite Charybdis.
Sirens	A pair of enchantresses who lure mariners with their song.
Scherie	Half-magical island of the Phaeacians.
Telemachus	Son of Odysseus and Penelope. He was only a baby when Odysseus left for Troy.
Teiresias	The old prophet of Thebes, who is consulted in the Underworld by Odysseus.
Ulysses	The Latin form of Odysseus' name.
Zeus	By far the most powerful of the family of gods on Olympus.

Picture Credits

Page 2 Johnny van Haeften Gallery, London (photo: Bridgeman Art Library); 12–13 MGM; 15 Kunsthaus, Zurich (photo: Swiss Institute for Art Research, Zurich); 17 Special Collections Dept., Northwestern University, Evanston, Illinois; 18 Kobal Collection; 20 David Messum (photo: Bridgeman Art Library); 21 Kunsthistorisches Museum, Vienna; 22 *top* National Gallery of Scotland, Edinburgh, *bottom* Cheek by Jowl/Robert Workman; 24 Gennadius Library, American School of Classical Studies, Athens; 28 British Museum; 30 National Museum of Athens (photo: Ekdotike Athenon SA); 31 from *Views in Greece* by Edward Dodwell, 1821; 32 Ashmolean Museum, Oxford; 43 National Library of Ireland, Dublin; 45 A & B Records; 48–9 *both* Bridgeman Art Library; 56 from *Description of the Plain of Troy* by M. Chevalier, translated by Andrew Dalzell 1791; 62 *top* British Museum, *bottom* Ecole des Beaux-Arts, Paris (photo: Giraudon); 66–7 Alte Pinakothek, Munich (photo: Joachim Blauel/Artothek); 70 National Gallery, London (photo: Bridgeman Art Library); 71 *top* Galleria Palatina, Florence (photo: Scala), *bottom* Ferens Art Gallery, Hull (photo: Bridgeman Art Library); 72 *top* Gennadius Library, American School of Classical Studies, Athens; 74–5 Johnny van Haeften Gallery, London (photo: Bridgeman Art Library); 76–7 *left* Forbes Magazine Collection, New York (photo: Bridgeman Art Library); 77 *top right* Öffentliche Kunstsammlung Basel, Kunstmuseum (photo: Colorphoto Hans Hinz); *bottom right* Kunsthaus, Zurich (photo: Swiss Institute for Art Research, Zurich); 80 *top* National Gallery, London, *bottom* Toledo Museum of Art, Ohio, gift of Edward Drummond Libbey; 82 Chris Davies; 83 from *A Vindication of Homer* by J. B. S. Morritt 1798; 84 Kunsthaus, Zurich (photo: Giraudon); 86 National Maritime Museum; 96 National Film Archive, London; 97 Popperfoto; 98 National Museum of Athens; 100 Agence de Presse Bernand; 101 Babette/Gordon Fraser Ltd; 102 British Library (photo: Bridgeman Art Library); 106 *top* British Museum, *bottom* Ashmolean Museum, Oxford; 109 *top* Palazzo Poggi, Bologna (photo: Scala), *bottom* Colorphoto Hans Hinz; 110 Ekdotike Athenon SA; 112 Ashmolean Museum, Oxford; 114 Bradford City Art Gallery (photo: Bridgeman Art Library); 115 Ancient Art & Architecture Collection; 117 Kunstmusuem, Aarau (photo: Swiss Institute for Art Research, Zurich); 118 © Succession Henri Matisse/DACS 1989 (photo: Phaidon Press Archives); 120 Dublin Civic Museum; 122–3 National Library of Ireland, Dublin; 124 Gilberton Company Inc., New York; 128 British Musuem; 131 Mansell Collection; 132 from *The Proceedings of the British School at Athens* 1937; 135 *right* John Hillelson Agency/Erich Lessing; 141 British Museum; 142 Vatican Museum (photo: Mansell Collection); 143 Metropolitan Museum of Art, New York, Fletcher Fund 1930; 145 Private collection (photo: Swiss Institute for Art Research, Zurich); 148 Mary Evans Picture Library; 150 Christie's; 151 Vorarlberger Landesmuseum, Bregenz; 153 Guy Gravett; 155 *top* Anvil Press; 156 from *The Stoic Comedians* by Hugh Kenner. W.H. Allen 1964; 158 Guy Gravett; 160 © ADAGP Paris/DACS London 1989 (photo: Sotheby's); 162 Koplin Gallery, Los Angeles; 163 from *The Odyssey: A Modern Sequel* by N. Kazantzakis 1938; 164 Phaidon Press Archives; 166 Biblioteca Marciana, Venice (photo: Giraudon); 167 Arlington Court (photo: National Trust).

The remaining photographs were taken by Beaty Rubens

Index

Numbers in italic refer to illustrations